THE AUTHOR

Dean Hayes took up full-time writing after a career in teaching and a spell as a professional cricketer. He has written over 80 sporting books, including *Scotland! Scotland! The Complete Who's Who of Scotland Players since 1945*, *Ireland's Greatest 300 Top Football Heroes* and *Living the Dream: Manchester City*.

CELTIC
100 HEROES

CELTIC
100 HEROES
of the MODERN GAME

Dean Hayes

MERCAT PRESS

First published in 2007 by Mercat Press
Birlinn Ltd, 10 Newington Road, Edinburgh EH9 1QS
www.mercatpress.com

ISBN-13: 978-1-84183-124-4
ISBN-10: 1-84183-124-7

Set in Ehrhardt with headings in Gill Sans at Mercat Press

Printed and bound in Great Britain by Antony Rowe Ltd

CONTENTS

ILLUSTRATIONS

INTRODUCTION

In this book I have attempted to capture the essence of the men who have made the biggest impact on the game in the post-war years. I was limited by consideration of space to profiles of 100 post-war Celtic players, and doubtless there will be readers who disagree with some of my final selections. But football is, after all, a game of opinions and herein are mine.

Celtic's history had already been long and glorious when Jock Stein, a former player of note, returned to Paradise (as the ground has always been colloquially known) to take charge in 1965. Under the authoritative eye of the Big Man, the club quickly transcended its Scottish origins to become an acknowledged power on the global scene, becoming the first British club to bring the European Cup to these shores. What is more, the League Championship win that proved their passport to glory, was just one of nine in a row from 1966 to 1974. This run of success set a Scottish record that has only recently been rivalled.

While Celtic have boasted in their ranks Republic of Ireland internationals like Packie Bonner, capped 80 times by his country, the playing staff in recent years has become more cosmopolitan than ever. That said, the famed Lisbon Lions who took European club football's ultimate prize in 1967 all came from within a 30-mile radius of Glasgow. Their willingness to work tirelessly for each other, combined with the defence-splitting skills of flying winger Jimmy Johnstone, proved too potent a combination for Inter Milan. A new wave of talent came through in the 70s, but the likes of Dalglish and Macari went on to make bigger names for themselves south of the Border. The pattern was repeated the following decade with Charlie Nicholas, while, in the 90s, the Bosman ruling let John Collins join Monaco without the Parkhead club receiving any recompense whatsoever. Two exceptions that proved the rule came in the form of Billy McNeill, the towering defender around whom Stein built his team and who would manage the club in two separate spells, and Paul McStay, long-time midfielder who refused to consider a move to Arsenal.

Despite an embarrassing start as manager, Gordon Strachan's Celtic side began to improve, and in his first season in charge, won the League Cup and the SPL in record time, with six matches remaining. The Hoops continued to flourish in 2006-7, and not only retained the title but progressed to the final 16 of the Champions League for the first time since the competition's restructure in 1993. Not surprisingly, Strachan was named the inaugural Scottish PFA Manager of the Year.

Football at Parkhead is a colourful cosmopolitan affair, even if the major players aren't necessarily there for the duration. One player who certainly made his mark over a period of years is Henrik Larsson, the free-scoring Swede whom Celtic fans took to their hearts.

There will inevitably be supporters who feel some players who have been omitted should have been included ahead of others. That is a matter for healthy debate. What is without doubt is that the players listed in the pages that follow helped build Glasgow Celtic into what it is today.

If, however, your personal player is missing, it might be that—in the tangle of justifications about who to include or exclude—they just missed out. Fear not, if your favourites are not here, they remain locked in the best place anyway—your heart.

Dean P. Hayes

DIDIER AGATHE

Born: Saint-Pierre, Reunion, France, 16 August 1975
Celtic career: 2000 to 2006
Appearances and goals:

League		FA Cup		Lg Cup		Europe	
A	G	A	G	A	G	A	G
111/11	9	16	0	4	0	32	3

Total appearances: 163/11
Total goals: 12
League Championships: 2000-01; 2001-02; 2003-04
Scottish Cup: 2000-01; 2003-04; 2004-05

Didier Agathe's rise to fame at Celtic elevated him to film-star status in his tiny homeland. The Parkhead midfielder became the most instantly recognisable personality on the sun-kissed Indian Ocean island of La Reunion. Following his visit to the island at the end of the club's treble-winning season of 2000-01, Agathe's face stared down at the 600,000 inhabitants from the billboards extolling his virtues as a footballer and highlighting the Parkhead club's success.

Agathe started out in France with Montpellier and also had a loan spell with Olympique Alès, but with his first team chances limited, he decided to try his luck in Scotland with Raith Rovers. Agathe moved to Starks Park on a free transfer in 1999 and enjoyed an impressive debut, scoring a hat-trick in a 4-1 win over Airdrie. Playing as a striker, his goals alerted Premier League club Hibernian, who signed him on a short-term contract.

He scored four goals in six appearances for Hibs before turning down the offer of a contract extension to join Glasgow Celtic for a reduced fee of around £50,000. He made his debut for the Bhoys in a 2-0 home win over St Mirren in October 2000, going on to help the club win the League Championship and the Scottish Cup in his first season with the club.

He continued to play an important part in Celtic's successes and appeared in all of the club's Champions League matches in 2001-02, scoring in the 3-1 away leg victory at Ajax. He was a member of the Celtic side that reached the 2003 UEFA Cup Final, only to lose 3-2 to Porto after extra-time. Martin O'Neill opted to play Agathe in an unusual right-back role for much of the 2003-04 campaign, but it didn't prevent him from netting twice in a 4-0 defeat of his former club Hibs at Easter Road. Despite a good start to the 2004-05 season, a returning groin injury kept Agathe out of action for six months from November to April. He made a brief return in January in a cup match against Rangers, but was sidelined again for an operation.

Throughout his time in Scotland, Agathe sent some of his earnings as a professional footballer back to his parents on the economically impoverished island of Reunion. It was his way of saying 'merci' for the emotional support which sustained him through the period of social repression and mental suffering he had to endure when he first arrived in France as a 16-year-old apprentice with Montpellier.

Having scarcely featured in 2005-06 under new manager Gordon Strachan, Agathe was linked with a number of clubs including Valencia, Juventus, Middlesbrough and Leeds United. However, no transfer was concluded by the end of the January 2006 transfer window and the following month an agreement was reached to terminate his contract with Celtic. In September 2006 he joined his former boss Martin O'Neill at Aston Villa on a short-term deal, but parted company with the club in early 2007 when the Midlands club chose not to extend his contract. Following an unsuccessful trial period with Nottingham Forest, at the time of writing he was currently seeking a club.

ROY AITKEN

Born: Irvine, 24 November 1958
Celtic career: 1975 to 1990
Appearances and goals:

League		FA Cup		Lg Cup		Europe	
A	G	A	G	A	G	A	G
483	40	55	4	82	6	47	5

Total appearances: 667
Total goals: 55
League Championships: 1976-77; 1978-79; 1980-81; 1981-82; 1985-86
Scottish Cup: 1976-77; 1979-80; 1984-85; 1987-88; 1988-89
League Cup: 1982 83
Honours: 57 Scotland caps

'That boy will play for Scotland one day,' was Jock Stein's remark after watching Roy Aitken play for the first time as a skinny 13-year-old. The youngster went on to prove the Big Man right, playing 57 times for his country—many of them as captain—during a glittering career which saw him turn out for the Hoops over three different decades!

He made his Celtic debut four years after his move to Parkhead from Ayr United Boys' Club, starring in a 2-0 win at Stenhousemuir in September 1975. Aitken established himself as a first team regular in the club's 1976-77 double-winning campaign, proving himself to be a hardworking midfielder with a never-say-die attitude.

Looked upon as the ideal replacement for Billy McNeill, Aitken was an inspirational leader, and once he got his name on the team-sheet, there was no way he was going to be dislodged. Unfortunately, his sometimes enthusiastic physical approach led to him receiving his marching orders on five occasions throughout his illustrious career. The first of these was

Roy Aitken playing in a Skol Cup semi-final against Aberdeen in 1984
(www.snspix.com)

as a 19-year-old when he had just been handed the captain's armband for a Scottish Cup tie against Kilmarnock at Rugby Park in 1978. He was also dismissed in the 1984 Scottish Cup Final clash with Aberdeen!

Aitken was a fixture in the Celtic side for 14 years, averaging over 40 games a term, and quickly became a firm favourite of the Parkhead fans. His uncompromising manner and sheer physical strength and presence earned him the nickname of 'The Bear'.

He was equally effective at full-back, central defence or sweeper, but it was in the holding role in front of Roddie MacDonald and later Tom McAdam, that Aitken was to prove his most valuable. He was a brilliant reader of the game, who could spot an opening long before it existed and with one telling pass, immediately turn defence into attack.

Two of his more memorable displays for the Bhoys came in games when he brought his side back from the brink of defeat to glorious victory. The first was the 1978-79 League Championship clincher against Rangers, and the second the 1985 Scottish Cup final victory over Dundee United, when it was his surge and cross that enabled Frank McGarvey to head home the winner. He led Celtic to the League and Cup double in their centenary season of 1987-88, and returned to Hampden the following season to retain the 'Blue Riband' against Rangers.

A regular for Scotland, he led his country in the 1986 World Cup Finals but was made the scapegoat for the 3-0 defeat by France in Paris in October 1989.

He had stated that he had wanted to end his playing days at Parkhead, but as the club's fortunes began to decline, he sought a transfer. He had appeared in 667 first team games for Celtic when in January 1990 he joined Newcastle United for a fee of £500,000. He made a remarkable debut for the Magpies, leading them to a 5-4 victory over Leicester City after they had been 4-2 down. His wholehearted displays almost took United to promotion, the Magpies failing in the play-offs. When Ossie Ardiles became Newcastle manager, he discarded Aitken when perhaps his vast experience was just what the St James Park club needed.

Aitken became player-manager at St Mirren, but after one season he moved to Aberdeen as the club's player-manager. Three years later he hung up his boots to concentrate on management, and in 1995-96 led the Dons to a League Cup Final success over Dundee. He was part of David O'Leary's backroom staff at Leeds United before following him to Villa Park, where, following O'Leary's dismissal, he was caretaker-manager. Aitken is now assistant to new Scotland manager Alex McLeish.

BERTIE AULD

Born: Maryhill, 23 March 1938
Celtic career: 1955 to 1961 and 1965 to 1971
Appearances and goals:

League		FA Cup		Lg Cup		Europe	
A	G	A	G	A	G	A	G
167/9	53	26/2	8	42/5	20	20/2	1

Total appearances: 255/18

Total goals: 82
League Championships: 1965-66; 1966-67; 1967-68; 1968-69; 1969-70
Scottish Cup: 1964-65; 1966-67; 1968-69
League Cup: 1966-67; 1967-68; 1968-69; 1969-70
European Cup: 1966-67
Honours: 3 Scotland caps

Though Jock Stein can rightly lay claim to turning a moderately talented bunch of players into the most skilful and feared side in Europe, it was the Big Man's predecessor who laid the foundations for the Parkhead club's meteoric rise, with the acquisition of former player Bertie Auld three

Bertie Auld in 1964 (www.snspix.com)

months before Stein's arrival in January 1965. He was certainly one of Celtic's greatest-ever signings, after Jimmy McGrory's right-hand man Sean Fallon persuaded the Celtic board to take a chance on a player who had been offloaded to Birmingham City four seasons earlier.

Before he made his Celtic debut, Auld spent much of the 1956-57 season on loan at Dumbarton. On his return to Parkhead, he made his debut against Rangers in a Glasgow cup-tie, but his early years with the club showed that he had an unfailing capacity for allowing himself to be goaded into misbehaviour. In fact, in that first spell with the club, Auld, who had played in the inter-League game against England, gained full international recognition. However, his temperament came into question when, on his international debut against Holland, he became only the second Scottish player to receive his marching orders.

In April 1961, Auld joined Birmingham City for a fee of £15,000, making his debut for the Midlands club in an Inter Cities Fairs Cup game against Inter Milan. He played in the first leg of the 1961 Fairs Cup Final against AS Roma and won a Football League Cup winners' tankard with the Blues in 1963, after Aston Villa had been beaten over two legs. Another couple of years passed before he returned to Parkhead for £12,000.

A player who could take two or three people out of the game with a pass, Bertie Auld possessed the sweetest left foot ever seen at Parkhead, and along with Bobby Murdoch formed the backbone of the side that was to dominate the game in Scotland for the best part of the next ten years. He was a genius with the ball, and his brace of goals in the 1965 Scottish Cup Final win over Dunfermline Athletic gave rise to the Stein era at Parkhead.

Auld helped win five Championships, three Scottish Cups, four League Cups and the European Cup in 1967, and it was the little midfielder who destroyed Fiorentina in Paradise three years later to set up the 'Battle of Britain' European Cup semi-final with Leeds United.

In 1971 he was rather surprisingly allowed to leave Celtic for Hibernian, a club he later managed without great success. Spells in charge of Partick Thistle (twice), Hamilton Academical and Dumbarton followed, before he called time on his football career late in 1988 to concentrate on running his Glasgow pub. However, there is little doubt that the years he spent with Celtic remain the most cherished of his memories, and affectionate recollection of them overcomes any bitterness he might feel about what happened anywhere else.

BOBO BALDE

Born: Marseille, France, 5 October 1975
Celtic career: 2001 to 2007
Appearances and goals:

League		FA Cup		Lg Cup		Europe	
A	G	A	G	A	G	A	G
156/1	9	14	2	14	5	45	0

Total appearances: 229/1
Total goals: 16
League Championships: 2001-02; 2003-04; 2005-06
Scottish Cup: 2003-04; 2004-05; 2006-07
League Cup: 2005-06
Honours: 8 Guinea caps

There are few players in the Scottish League, or indeed European football, who provide as considerable presence in defence as Guinean international Bobo Balde.

One of 12 children, he started out with his home-town team, Marseille, in 1995, but on being unable to break into the first team, left to join Second Division outfit FC Mulhouse prior to the start of the 1997-98 season. Despite him being an instant hit, the club were relegated and he moved on to AS Cannes, where he had little success before transferring to Toulouse FC, whom he helped to promotion during the 1999-2000 season. Although their stay in the top flight was brief, it was long enough to alert Celtic to his defensive capabilities.

Balde made his debut for the Hoops in a 3-1 home win over Dunfermline Athletic in September 2001, and a few games later netted his first goal for the club, also at Parkhead, against Dundee United. A ferocious tackler and not afraid of getting forward, he helped the club win the League Championship and also found the net in the Scottish Cup Final against Rangers, but the Light Blues won 3-2.

He was booked in the first Old Firm game of the 2002-03 season, which ended all-square at 3-3, but at the end of the campaign he was named Celtic Player of the Year by the Hoops fans. He played in 12 of Celtic's 13 UEFA Cup games as Celtic reached the final, where their opponents in the Olympic Stadium in Seville were FC Porto. During the match, Balde was sent off in the 5th minute of extra time after picking up his second booking. Celtic went down 3-2 with Henrik Larsson getting both of the club's goals.

At the end of the following season, Balde, who was a rock at the heart of the Celtic defence, added another League Championship and a Scottish Cup medal to his collection, but was sadly subjected to chants of monkey noises from sections of the Rangers supporters during a Scottish Cup game at Parkhead towards the end of that 2003-04 campaign. The following season he netted a couple of goals in a 3-0 home win over Dundee, coming close to netting his first-ever hat-trick. He added another Scottish Cup medal to his collection when Alan Thompson's free-kick was enough to defeat Dundee United in the final.

Although French by birth, he, along with Celtic team-mate Mohammed Sylla, both play international football for Guinea. Balde made his debut during the 2002 African Nations Cup. He was part of the 2004 side that reached the quarter-finals before losing to Mali, and was a regular in the 2006 World Cup qualifying matches. He has also helped Guinea to the quarter-finals of the African Cup of Nations for the last two Championships.

The 2005-06 season was another successful one for Balde, this in spite of him getting booked in both legs of the 5-4 aggregate defeat by Artmedia Bratislava. He scored once in the emphatic 3-0 victory over Rangers as Celtic went on to win the Scottish Premier League and League Cup. He missed the start of the 2006-07 season after discovering he required surgery for a persistent stomach muscle problem. He returned to first team action in November, only to suffer a broken leg in the game against Dundee United on Boxing Day.

PACKIE BONNER

Born: Clochglas, near Kincasslagh, Co. Donegal, 24 May 1960
Celtic career: 1978 to 1996
Appearances and goals:

League		FA Cup		Lg Cup		Europe	
A	G	A	G	A	G	A	G
483	0	55	0	64	0	40	0

Total appearances: 642
Total goals: 0
League Championships: 1980-81; 1981-82; 1985-86; 1987-88
Scottish Cup: 1984-85; 1988-89; 1994-95
League Cup: 1982-83
Honours: 80 Republic of Ireland caps

Jock Stein's eye for spotting real talent was legendary, and Bonner became the Big Man's last signing when he joined the Hoops in May 1978. Along with Willie Miller and Ronnie Simpson, Packie Bonner is considered the greatest of Celtic's post-war goalkeepers.

Bonner, who was also a highly-rated Gaelic footballer, was spotted playing soccer for Leicester City's youth team, and very little persuasion was required to entice him over from his home in Co. Donegal. He made his debut on St Patrick's Day 1979 in a 2-1 victory over Motherwell, and a year later he had displaced Peter Latchford as the club's regular keeper. Not always blessed with the cream of the defensive world in front of him, Packie—a master shot-stopper with few peers in a one-on-one situation—

Packie Bonner in a game against Dundee in 1992 (www.snspix.com)

went on to win four League Championship medals, three Scottish Cup medals and a League Cup medal in a career which saw him turn out for the club on well over 600 occasions.

However, it will probably be for his heroics at international level that Bonner will best be remembered. Having won caps for the Republic of Ireland at youth and Under-21 level, he was called into the senior squad for a tour of Germany and Poland in the summer of 1981. He made his full international debut on his 21st birthday in the game against Poland. The arrival of Jack Charlton as Republic of Ireland team manager in 1986 proved the watershed in the international career of Packie Bonner. He missed just one of the Republic's qualifying matches ahead of the 1988 European Championships, and despite missing Celtic's 1988 Scottish Cup Final victory over Dundee United due to injury, played in each of the country's three matches during the tournament finals. His performance in the defeat of England in Stuttgart—especially the save late on to deny Gary Lineker—was memorable.

In the 1990 World Cup Finals in Italy, Bonner conceded just two goals in the group matches, but it was his display in the second round tie against Romania for which he will always be remembered. After two hours of football, the game remained goalless and went to a penalty shoot-out. After each team had successfully converted four spot-kicks, the weary Bonner produced a superb save to deny Romania's Daniel Timofte. Although the Irish lost out to the hosts in the quarter-finals, Bonner was brilliant and unlucky to concede the game's only goal after making an excellent save from Donadoni.

Back at club level, Bonner was dropped by Liam Brady and then given a free transfer by his successor Lou Macari. He was, however, persuaded to stay, although a little pressure was needed, when new boss Tommy Burns took over the reins months later. He then crowned a glorious goalkeeping career at Parkhead with a clean sheet in the 1995 Scottish Cup Final triumph over Airdrie.

Packie was subsequently a coach at Parkhead and, later, Reading, before in February 2003, being named as technical director and goalkeeping coach for the Football Association of Ireland under Brian Kerr. He did not keep this position when Kerr was sacked and replaced with Steve Staunton. In addition he has worked as a football presenter with TV3 Ireland.

ARTUR BORUC

Born: Sledice, Poland, 20 February 1980
Celtic career: 2005 to 2007
Appearances and goals:

League		FA Cup		Lg Cup		Europe	
A	G	A	G	A	G	A	G
73	0	6	0	6	0	9	0

Total appearances: 94
Total goals: 0
League Championships: 2005-06; 2006-07
Scottish Cup: 2006-07
League Cup: 2005-06
Honours: 29 Poland caps

Polish international goalkeeper Artur Boruc moved to Celtic on what was originally a year-long loan from Legia Warsaw in the summer of 2005. However, after nine games the deal was made permanent in October of that year, with Boruc penning a three-and-a-half year deal.

On coming to the club, Boruc said 'I want to be No.1 with Celtic and with Poland and win myself a longer contract here. If I play over here then Jerzy Dudek will have a little problem over in Liverpool.' The 'little problem' that Boruc referred to was who would play in goal for Poland in the 2006 World Cup in Germany. As it transpired, Dudek's lack of matches for Liverpool resulted in it becoming a one-horse race.

Boruc introduced himself to the Celtic supporters with a penalty save in the opening minute of his debut against Leicester City. He made his SPL debut for the Hoops in a 2-0 home win over Dundee United and went from strength to strength. He kept 14 clean sheets in all games, and kept hold of the No.1 jersey until David Marshall was given three games in the final month of the season with the title already won.

As well as helping the Hoops win the League title, he was between the posts when Celtic beat Dunfermline Athletic 3-0 to win the League Cup. An athletic shot-stopper and genuine personality on and off the park, Boruc was selected to the 23-man Poland squad for the 2006 World Cup Finals. He had been battling with Tomasz Kuszczak for the starting slot, but was first-choice goalkeeper during the tournament. Boruc was in outstanding form and one of the few positives in what was a disappointing campaign for the Poles.

Boruc, who makes the sign of the cross before every game as part of a good-luck ritual, was cautioned by Strathclyde Police for a breach of the peace for making gestures in front of Rangers fans. According to the *Sunday Herald* 'police reports highlighted three hand gestures made by the Pole... a v-sign at the crowd, another obscene gesture at the crowd and a blessing'. The gestures were not caught on video and the caution was issued on the basis of police reports and witness statements.

On 21 November 2006, in a Champions League match against Manchester United at Parkhead, Boruc helped Celtic through to the knockout stage of the competition by saving Louis Saha's 89th minute penalty.

The following month he was named as 'Player of the Month' in the SPL, but in the first Old Firm game since the caution, he again crossed himself, drawing a roar from the Rangers fans behind his goal. A spokesman for Celtic defended his gesture, stating 'the police have said they have no problem with Artur Boruc in this regard and neither does Celtic Football Club'.

TOMMY BOYD

Born: Glasgow, 24 November 1965
Celtic career: 1992 to 2003
Appearances and goals:

League		FA Cup		Lg Cup		Europe	
A	G	A	G	A	G	A	G
296/10	2	31/3	0	31/2	0	33/1	0

Total appearances: 391/16
Total goals: 2
League Championships: 1997-98; 2000-01
Scottish Cup: 1994-95; 2000-01
League Cup: 1997-98; 1999-2000; 2000-01
Honours: 72 Scotland caps

Very little of Liam Brady's time in charge of Celtic will be remembered with affection, but the acquisition of Tommy Boyd certainly bucked the trend of his two-year tenure.

The cultured left-back already had a Scottish Cup winners' medal and over 250 appearances for Motherwell behind him when he left to join Chelsea, following his side's 1991 success over Dundee United. It was only the second time that Motherwell had lifted the country's top knockout trophy. But that was to be his last appearance for the Lanarkshire club as the Stamford Bridge club paid £800,000 for his services.

There is no doubt that Tommy Boyd made his reputation at Motherwell, where his incisive play and shrewd thinking won him many admirers, and he won international recognition at full international level, having played for Scotland at both 'B' and Under-21 level. His international career later brought him membership of the SFA's Hall of Fame, reserved for those with over 50 national caps. He played his part in two trips to European Championship Finals and the 1998 World Cup Finals.

Boyd failed to settle with the Londoners, and his unhappy eight-month stay, which saw him play just 23 times, was ended when Brady agreed a swap deal with counterpart Ian Porterfield for Parkhead misfit Tony Cascarino.

Boyd was revealed as a masterful playmaker, comfortable with either foot and an instant hit with the fans of the club he supported as a boy. Ironically, during his first season with Celtic, Boyd made his first return to Fir Park, where he conceded a penalty and was sent off for fouling Motherwell's Dougie Arnott!

However, success did follow for Boyd, who was converted to the right side of defence by new boss Tommy Burns, when he picked up his second Scottish Cup winners' medal following the 1-0 defeat of Airdrie at Hampden in May 1995. As Jackie McNamara and Tosh McKinlay arrived to fill the full-back berths, Boyd formed a positively Scrooge-like partnership with

Celtic stars Tommy Boyd (left), Jackie McNamara and Tommy Johnson (right) celebrate the win over Aberdeen in the 2000 CIS Cup Final (www.snspix.com)

John Hughes at the heart of the Hoops defence. With the later arrival of Alan Stubbs, Boyd—who had few peers when it came to the reading of a game—moved back to sweeper-cum-libero role, a position where he looked extremely comfortable.

Boyd gained the captaincy from the recently retired Paul McStay, and was part of the Celtic side built by Wim Jansen that broke Rangers' stranglehold on the League title in 1997-98, and was also around when Martin O'Neill did the same for two seasons.

A dedicated professional with a long and distinguished career, Tommy Boyd carried out his job with total reliability and received a testimonial against Manchester United in 2001 after 10 seasons of sterling service to the cause of Celtic Football Club. He also received the MBE in the Queen's Birthday Honours list in the summer of 2002, for services to football, prior to retiring the following year.

JIM BROGAN

Born: Glasgow, 5 June 1944
Celtic career: 1963 to 1975
Appearances and goals:

League		FA Cup		Lg Cup		Europe	
A	**G**	**A**	**G**	**A**	**G**	**A**	**G**
213	6	38	0	57	2	31	1

Total appearances: 339
Total goals: 9
League Championships: 1967-68; 1968-69; 1969-70; 1970-71; 1971-72; 1972-73; 1973-74
Scottish Cup: 1968-69; 1970-71; 1971-72; 1974-75
League Cup: 1968-69; 1969-70; 1974-75
Honours: 4 Scotland caps

Jim Brogan was a stylish defender who was always overshadowed by the bigger names in the Celtic team at the time he played. He was unfortunate in that he came into the Hoops line-up at the time when players of the calibre of Kenny Dalglish, George Connelly, Danny McGrain and Lou Macari were all making their names.

Having made his Celtic debut at Falkirk in September 1963, Brogan served quite a lengthy apprenticeship before becoming a first team regular at Parkhead, succeeding John Clark in the No.6 shirt, and was in fact, rather older than the aforementioned wave of players who replaced the Lisbon Lions. Considered a first team regular by manager Jock Stein in the late 1960s and early 1970s, he picked up a number of domestic honours before being given a free transfer in 1975.

Brogan, who was named runner-up to Martin Buchan in the 1971 Scottish Player of the Year award, fitted the Celtic mould at left-half and enjoyed cantering up the park to join the attack when he could. As George Connelly later laid claim to his position, he moved to left-back to enjoy two more successful seasons and pick up a fourth Scottish Cup medal.

A Celtic fan as a boy, Jim Brogan was recognised by the Parkhead faithful as one of them and was always a great favourite with the club's supporters. He was good enough to play for the Scottish League against their English counterparts in 1969, and won full international honours for Scotland the following year. Sadly, his fourth and last appearance for the national side—against England at Wembley—saw him sustain a broken leg, and he was unable to reclaim his international place.

Though he didn't score too many goals from his position at left-back or left-half, he did pop up in the penalty area to head a last-gasp winner for the Hoops against Rangers in January 1972.

Having won seven League Championship medals, four Scottish Cup medals and three League Cup medals, and captaining the Celtic team in his final match against arch-enemies Rangers in May 1975—a game to celebrate

Glasgow's 800th birthday—he left Parkhead on a free transfer to play for Coventry City. He spent just one season at Highfield Road before returning to Scotland to see out his career with Ayr United.

Brogan, who later became a hugely successful businessman with a million-pound empire, might well have made the Parkhead club an excellent Chief Executive in the early 1990s.

CRAIG BURLEY

Born: Irvine, 24 September 1971
Celtic career: 1997 to 1999
Appearances and goals:

League		FA Cup		Lg Cup		Europe	
A	**G**	**A**	**G**	**A**	**G**	**A**	**G**
61/3	20	6	0	7	0	12	1

Total appearances: **86/3**
Total goals: **21**
League Championships: 1997-98
League Cup: 1997-98
Honours: 46 Scotland caps

A nephew of George Burley, the former Ipswich star and current manager of Southampton, he was voted Scottish Premier League Player of the Year for season 1997-98 by the Scottish Football Writers' Association.

Midfielder Burley started his career with Chelsea, where he was a bit-part player in his early days at Stamford Bridge. Even so, within a week of making his full debut for Chelsea, he was selected to represent Scotland at Under-21 level. He suffered more than his fair share of injuries with the London club, but gradually became a key player for player-manager Glenn Hoddle and later Ruud Gullit.

Having impressed Craig Brown, he became an integral part of the Scottish squad for Euro '96, later featuring in the bizarre World Cup qualifier against Estonia in Tallinn when Scotland's opposition failed to turn up and the game was abandoned after three seconds!

Burley won his first medal in 1997, being part of the Chelsea team that beat Middlesbrough 2-0 in the FA Cup Final at Wembley. However, during the summer, he signed for Celtic, becoming one of Wim Jansen's first signings at the club.

The £3.25 million signing had a good first season at Parkhead, helping the Hoops to break Rangers' dominance. He netted 13 goals from midfield, helping Celtic lift both the League Championship and the League Cup, beating Dundee United 3-0 in the final. He started the following campaign by netting an opening day hat-trick in a 5-0 defeat of Dunfermline Athletic, and scored two further goals in the opening few matches against Dundee

United and Dundee. Celtic finished the season as runners-up to Rangers, but, surprisingly, lost to Airdrie in the third round of the League Cup, and rivals Rangers in the final of the Scottish Cup.

After an unhappy start to the 1999-2000 season, Burley left Parkhead to join Derby County after manager Jim Smith paid £3 million for his signature. His impact at Pride Park was immediate, and he and Georgian international Kinkladze were instrumental in the Rams retaining their top flight status. Despite County's poor form the following season, Burley remained a regular for both club and country until suffering a serious injury in a match against Newcastle in 2001. He didn't play for a further year, missing Derby's relegation season.

On regaining full fitness, he announced his retirement from international football, blasting manager Berti Vogts in the process. Released by Derby in the summer of 2003, the same happened with his next club Dundee after the club went into administration. After spells with Preston North End and Walsall, Burley abruptly retired at only 32, citing as the reason that he was fed up with football.

Burley has recently become a TV pundit with the media company Setanta Sports.

TOMMY BURNS

Born: Glasgow, 16 December 1956
Celtic career: 1975 to 1989
Appearances and goals:

League		FA Cup		Lg Cup		Europe	
A	**G**	**A**	**G**	**A**	**G**	**A**	**G**
324/32	52	38/5	12	70/1	15	32/3	4

Total appearances: 464/41
Total goals: 83
League Championships: 1976-77; 1978-79; 1980-81; 1981-82; 1985-86; 1987-88
Scottish Cup: 1979-80; 1984-85; 1987-88; 1988-89
League Cup: 1982-83
Honours: 8 Scotland caps

Tommy Burns only ever had one ambition in life, and that was to play for Celtic. Growing up in the tough Calton district of the East End of Glasgow, the fiery redheaded midfielder could never have imagined that he would one day manage the side he had dreamed of playing for.

He played for Eastercraigs and Maryhill FC before making the grade with Celtic. Having made his debut for the Hoops as a substitute for Paul Wilson in a 2-1 defeat against Dundee in April 1975, he soon established himself as a first team regular at Parkhead.

A superbly gifted midfielder, with the sweetest left foot seen at Parkhead

Tommy Burns thanks the heavens after scoring in the penalty shoot-out to decide the semi-final of the Scottish League Cup against Motherwell in 1986. Celtic won this match but not the Cup (www.snspix.com)

since the days of Bertie Auld, Burns had the ability to prise open any opposition defence with a precision pass or mazy dribble which, in full flight, was reminiscent of the great Jimmy Johnstone in his heyday. However, in his early days with the club he seemed to be continually clashing with authority, and, in a little over a year, he received three red cards.

His attitude, however, turned full circle and from then on, he never retaliated no matter how intense the provocation—this included being punched in the face by Hearts' John Robertson and Kienast of Rapid Vienna.

During his time with Celtic, he was rewarded with six League Championship medals, four Scottish Cup winners' medals and a League Cup winners' medal. The fact that he accrued only eight international caps for Scotland remains a mystery, amplified by the fact that Jock Stein, who brought the skinny little teenager to Parkhead, was in charge of the national side when Tommy Burns was at the peak of his career.

He departed for Kilmarnock in December 1989 after affectionately donating his boots to the Jungle following his last game for Celtic against Ajax. He became Killie's player-manager in 1992, winning the club promotion to the Premier Division in 1992-93. Shortly afterwards, he was summoned 'home' to pick up the pieces following the disastrous reigns of Liam Brady and Lou Macari.

In the fans' eyes, Tommy Burns was the only candidate for the job. But the surrender of the club's cherished nine-in-a-row record to their greatest rivals Rangers in 1997 brought a premature end to his stay in Paradise. Supporters wept openly as he walked out of Parkhead, many feeling a grave sense of injustice that he had not been given enough time to finish the job.

He then went to work under Kenny Dalglish at Newcastle United, and later moved on to an undistinguished period of management at Reading. He became assistant-manager of Scotland under Berti Vogts and retained the position under Walter Smith. He returned to Celtic for a third time when Martin O'Neill placed him in charge of youth development. In January 2007, Burns announced through Celtic's official website that he was severing all ties with the Scottish national team to concentrate on his role at the club.

JORGE CADETE

Born: Pemba, Mozambique, 27 August 1968
Celtic career: 1996 to 1997
Appearances and goals:

League		FA Cup		Lg Cup		Europe	
A	G	A	G	A	G	A	G
32/5	30	5	2	5	1	3	1

Total appearances: 45/5
Total goals: 34

Though Portuguese international Jorge Cadete's only full season with the Hoops was 1996-97, it was the greatest of his career.

He began his footballing career with Associacao Academica de Santarem in 1983-84, aged just 15, scoring an amazing 43 goals in just 18 games. His exploits alerted Portuguese giants Sporting and Benfica, with the former winning the race for his signature. Sent out on loan to Vitoria Setubal to gain experience, his skill quickly brought him back to Sporting. However, his only piece of silverware came during 1995 when he won the Portuguese Cup 2-0 against Maritimo.

He became unsettled with life at Sporting and joined Brescia Calcio on loan in November 1994. After a year he rejoined Sporting, but it was clear his future did not lie there.

In April 1996, after a lengthy transfer wrangle, Cadete's contract was rescinded and he signed for Celtic on a free transfer. His debut came against Aberdeen at Parkhead, where he came off the bench to score Celtic's fifth goal in a 5-0 victory. Cadete became an instant hit with the Celtic faithful.

His transfer to Celtic, though, was controversial. Despite being signed prior to the transfer deadline, the SFA delayed processing his registration in time for a Scottish Cup tie against Rangers at Ibrox. Following a complaint from Celtic chairman Fergus McCann, SFA chief Jim Farry was relieved of his duties after being found guilty of deliberately holding back Jorge Cadete's registration.

Cadete finished the following season, 1996-97, as Scotland's top goalscorer, with 33 goals in 44 appearances in all competitions, and, to his immense pride, without the aid of penalty-kicks. Despite this, the Hoops lost out on the League title to arch-rivals Rangers. Cadete netted a hat-trick in the 6-0 defeat of Kilmarnock and another treble in the League Cup tie against Alloa, which Celtic won 5-1. Cadete played his last match for Celtic against Dundee United at the end of the season, when he bowed to the Celtic fans before kissing the turf, sparking rumours of an imminent departure.

Celtic boss Tommy Burns made way for new coach Wim Jansen, and Cadete remained a Celtic player throughout the close season. Then, citing mental health issues and a failure to adjust to life in Scotland without his family, he requested a transfer. After failing to show for pre-season training, he was transferred to La Liga outfit Celta Vigo for £3.5 million. Along with Di Canio and Pierre van Hooijdonk, Cadete was labelled as one of the 'Three Amigos' by Celtic chairman Fergus McCann.

After a season with Celta Vigo, he joined Benfica along with former Celtic strike partner Van Hooijdonk. He later had a spell on loan with Premiership new boys Bradford City, but failed to win a permanent move and signed for Estrela da Amadora. Following his release he was unable to find a new club and retired at the age of 33, going on to make an appearance on the celebrity version of the Big Brother reality TV show.

At the age of 35 he opted for a move back to Scottish football with Partick Thistle, but the move was controversial as he had agreed to sign for Raith Rovers, even being photographed in the team shirt by the media. He made his debut against Celtic and was jeered as he came off the bench by Celtic fans, who recalled the manner of his departure from Celtic six years previously. A shadow of his former self, he was subsequently not offered a contract extension.

STEVE CHALMERS

Born: Glasgow, 26 December 1936
Celtic career: 1959 to 1971
Appearances and goals:

League		FA Cup		Lg Cup		Europe	
A	G	A	G	A	G	A	G
253/10	156	45/2	29	57/3	31	37/1	13

Total appearances: 392/16
Total goals: 229
League Championships: 1965-66; 1966-67; 1967-68; 1968-69
Scottish Cup: 1964-65; 1966-67; 1968-69
League Cup: 1966-67; 1967-68; 1968-69; 1969-70
European Cup: 1966-67
Honours: 5 Scotland caps

Steve Chalmers enjoyed many highs while wearing the famous hoops, but it will be for one golden moment in Lisbon in 1967 that he is most fondly remembered by Celtic fans. Chalmers earned his rightful place in the record books with the 85th minute goal that finally ended the dogged resistance of Inter Milan in the famous European Cup Final victory of that year.

His father had played alongside Jimmy McGrory at Clydebank in the 1920s, while his son Paul made a few appearances for Celtic in the mid-1980s.

Born on Boxing Day 1936, Chalmers began his career with Kirkintilloch Rob Roy, but, unfortunately, while there, he was in hospital for six months and out of the game for over a year with meningitis. He then joined top non-League club Ashfield, where he represented his country at junior level before arriving at Parkhead in February 1959.

Often used as an orthodox winger on either side of the park, he had pace and an eye for goal, but it was not until he was switched to his favoured centre-forward role by Jock Stein that the best of the likeable hitman was seen.

Steve Chalmers takes the ball round Airdrie goalkeeper Roddy McKenzie in a 1966 match (www.snspix.com)

Chalmers won five full international caps for Scotland, including a memorable 1-1 draw against Brazil in 1966 which saw him get his name on the scoresheet for the first time with a first-minute goal.

One of Steve Chalmers' greatest moments came in the semi-final of the European Cup in Prague during that 1966-67 season, when, as Celtic's only forward, he seemed to cover every blade of grass. Having netted a second-half hat-trick in a 5-1 defeat of arch-rivals Rangers in January 1966, a wonderful goal in the 4-0 Scottish Cup Final drubbing of the same opponents cemented his position as an idol of the Parkhead faithful—but just five months later, his career suffered an almost fatal knock when he broke his leg in the 1969 League Cup Final victory over St Johnstone.

He then found it difficult to regain his place in the Celtic side, and in 1971 joined Morton. He moved to Partick Thistle the following year. At this time he owned a licensed grocers in the Maryhill district and subsequently worked for the successful Celtic Development Pools agency.

A keen photographer and golfer, his total of goals for the Hoops in all competitions was a post-war club record, until surpassed by Bobby Lennox in November 1973.

JOHN CLARK

Born: Bellshill, 13 March 1941
Celtic career: 1958 to 1971
Appearances and goals:

League		FA Cup		Lg Cup		Europe	
A	**G**	**A**	**G**	**A**	**G**	**A**	**G**
175/10	1	30/1	1	60/2	1	39/1	0

Total appearances: 304/14
Total goals: 3
League Championships: 1965-66; 1966-67; 1967-68
Scottish Cup: 1964-65; 1966-67; 1968-69
League Cup: 1965-66; 1966-67; 1967-68; 1968-69
European Cup: 1966-67
Honours: 4 Scotland caps

Regarded by most Celtic fans as a quiet achiever, John Clark was a central defender of real quality, but one who shunned the limelight in favour of being a vital cog in Celtic's greatest-ever side.

Today, when people speak of the Lisbon Lions, names such as Tommy Gemmell, Jimmy Johnstone and Billy McNeill trip off many a tongue. However, John Clark was coolly efficient and equally important. Older fans believe the legendary Billy McNeill would never have been half the player he was had Clark not been around to cover his back.

Clark joined Celtic from Larkhall Thistle in 1958 and began his career in the hoops as a traditional left-half, making his debut in a 5-0 win at Arbroath in October 1959. However, Stein recognised the player's strengths and understanding of the game and immediately installed him as a sweeper— hence his nickname 'The Brush'.

It was not until the spring of 1961, however, that he began to push his way into the first team on a regular basis, replacing the ageing Bertie Peacock. In a tense Scottish Cup quarter-final replay, Clark scored the extra-time winner for Celtic against Hibs at Easter Road—one of only three goals in a lengthy Celtic career—and as a result he was preferred to Peacock in the disastrous Scottish Cup Final and replay against Jock Stein's Dunfermline of that year.

From 1961 to the arrival of Stein, Clark played sporadically, quite often out of position. He was out of favour in 1963 and so missed the horrors of the Rangers Cup Finals of that year, but was then quite clearly on the wrong side of the Clark, McNeill and Kennedy half-back line. Following Stein's arrival, he lined up in a 'flat back four' of Craig, McNeill, Clark and Gemmell—a role in which he was superb, always on hand when McNeill got a little flustered!

Apart from his Lisbon heroics, Clark won three League Championships, three Scottish Cup winners' medals and four League Cup winners' medals.

However, he was the first of the Lisbon Lions to be supplanted by a younger man—in his case, Jim Brogan.

In 1971 Clark left to join Morton, but retired from playing soon after. He re-entered the game as assistant-manager at Aberdeen and later Celtic between 1978 and 1983 as Billy McNeill's right-hand man—as he had been on the pitch for many years. He later managed Cowdenbeath, Stranraer and Clyde, but perhaps lacked the flair and charisma to be a manager.

In recent years, he has been the kit manager at Celtic, a job that he seems very happy with. He is after all working for the Hoops, a club that he loves and one that means so much to him and in whose history he played such a glorious part.

BOBBY COLLINS

Born: Glasgow, 16 February 1931
Celtic career: 1949 to 1958
Appearances and goals:

League		FA Cup		Lg Cup		Europe	
A	**G**	**A**	**G**	**A**	**G**	**A**	**G**
220	81	38	10	62	26	-	-

Total appearances: 320
Total goals: 117
League Championships: 1953-54
Scottish Cup: 1950-51
League Cup: 1956-57; 1957-58
Honours: 31 Scotland caps

Midfield general Bobby Collins belied his diminutive stature with a towering talent. His departure from Parkhead after ten years with the club—the proceeds of his sale, it is rumoured, going to pay for new floodlights—was much mourned, but it was perhaps in the twilight of his career that he made his greatest mark as captain of Don Revie's great Leeds United side of the 1960s.

Originally a winger when he arrived at Parkhead, it was when he moved to inside-forward that Collins exerted his greatest influence on the game. Collins was also an ice-cool penalty-taker, scoring a unique hat-trick of them in September 1953 against Aberdeen. His skill with the dead ball was further illustrated by his legendary 'one-step' corner kicks, delivered accurately with scarcely a run up. His size-4 boots were amongst the smallest in first-class soccer, yet they packed an astonishingly powerful shot.

Collins received international recognition as early as April 1950, when he was picked by Scotland to play against Switzerland at Hampden, but he strained a leg in a friendly fixture and was forced to miss the game.

However, the following autumn, he did win the first of 31 caps when the Scots beat Wales 3-1.

Having helped Celtic to many honours in the 1950s, kicking off with the Scottish Cup win of 1950-51, he was a key ingredient of the double-winning team of 1953-54, despite missing the Cup Final itself. He also won League Cup medals in 1956-57 and 1957-58.

In September 1958 Collins was transferred to Everton for £23,000, and for two seasons was arguably the major factor in the Merseyside club retaining their top flight status. Nicknamed 'the Little General', he left Goodison Park in March 1962, with Leeds United paying £25,000 for his services.

His supreme talent helped transform the Yorkshire club from a mediocre Second Division side into a powerful force in Division One. After captaining Leeds to the Second Division title, Collins was voted English Footballer of the Year in 1965 as United narrowly failed to take the double—missing out on the League title to Manchester United on goal difference and losing the FA Cup Final to Liverpool. He was also recalled to the Scottish national side after a six-year absence.

A broken thigh sustained in a European Cup game against Torino in October 1965 was hard to overcome at nearly 35, and he left Elland Road on a free transfer to join Bury. He stayed at Gigg Lane for two years, leading the Shakers into the Second Division. He then had a short spell back in Scottish football with Morton, and was player-coach in Australia before starring for Shamrock Rovers and finally Oldham Athletic.

The 'Wee Barra' has since managed Huddersfield Town, Hull City and Barnsley, and while boss at non-League Guiseley Town, shared a testimonial with John Charles in honour of his Leeds United days. On leaving the game, he spent eight years working in the wholesale fashion business, prior to working as a chauffeur at Leeds University garage—this while playing in the occasional charity game.

JOHN COLLINS

Born: Galashiels, 31 January 1968
Celtic career: 1990 to 1996
Appearances and goals:

League		FA Cup		Lg Cup		Europe	
A	G	A	G	A	G	A	G
211/6	47	21	3	22	3	13	1

Total appearances: 267/6
Total goals: 54
Scottish Cup: 1994-95
Honours: 58 Scotland caps

Celtic were forced to pay Hibernian £920,000 to bring gifted midfielder

John Collins is shadowed by Pieter Huistra in a 1991 Old Firm game in the Premier Division (www.snspix.com)

John Collins back to Parkhead in the summer of 1990, after letting him slip through the net as a raw 16-year-old. Born in Galashiels, Collins gained rave reviews for his performances with Celtic Boys Club before he was, surprisingly, allowed to leave for non-League Hutcheson Vale. From there he was promptly snapped up by Hibs in 1984.

Collins established himself in the Easter Road club's first team the following season, and his superb vision and close control soon had scouts from the country's leading clubs filling the stands week in, week out. International recognition soon followed for a player whose ball-winning skills and lethal long-range shooting tempted Celtic boss Billy McNeill to part with nearly £1 million when the player arrived home from the World Cup Finals in 1990.

Collins soon formed a telepathic understanding with international team-mate Paul McStay, but a lack of class forwards in front of them frequently saw the pair's best efforts count for nothing. One of his most memorable displays for the Hoops came against Cologne in the UEFA Cup first round second leg. Celtic started 2-0 down, but Collins ran amok and the Bhoys took the tie 3-2 on aggregate. Sadly, during his time at Parkhead, he was restricted to just one domestic honour—when he skippered the side to success in the Scottish Cup Final of 1995 over Airdrie—and he decided to head for pastures new.

The arrival of top Europeans Pierre van Hooijdonk, Jorge Cadete and Andreas Thom failed to persuade him that the good times were just around the corner at Parkhead, and, as a free agent, he headed for AS Monaco in the summer of 1996. His departure from Parkhead was far from harmonious, although the fans' anger was directed more at the club for failing to offer Collins a deal that could have tempted him to stay.

Collins, an arch-critic of the often bruising nature of Scottish football, revelled in the time and space afforded to him in the French First Division, and a Championship medal was captured in his first season in the Principality. The next season saw Monaco reach the European Cup semi-final, defeating Manchester United in the quarter-final. Collins returned to these shores in the summer of 1998 by moving to Walter Smith's Everton.

After having a penalty saved on his Everton home debut, tragedy struck when a niggling injury hampered his performances and eventually forced him to undergo surgery midway through the 1998-99 campaign. Once he had recovered he moved to Jean Tigana's Fulham for £2 million, and in his first season at Craven Cottage he led the London club to the First Division Championship.

After retiring from football, he obtained a number of coaching qualifications, including the UEFA Pro Licence. He retained his links with his former clubs, and when Fulham signed a new player in 2004, it was John Collins who introduced Collins John!

In October 2006, Collins was appointed manager of Hibernian, leading the Edinburgh side to the League Cup Final where they beat Kilmarnock 5-1, and in doing so, secured the club's first piece of silverware in 16 years and his own first success as a manager.

GEORGE CONNELLY

Born: Fife, I March 1949
Celtic career: 1964 to 1975
Appearances and goals:

League		FA Cup		Lg Cup		Europe	
A	G	A	G	A	G	A	G
129/7	5	24/1	2	60/3	4	28/2	2

Total appearances: 241/13
Total goals: 13
League Championships: 1970-71; 1971-72; 1972-73; 1973-74
Scottish Cup: 1968-69; 1970-71; 1971-72;
Honours: 2 Scotland caps

The sight of George Connelly stroking the ball into an empty Hampden net in April 1969 will be forever etched in the minds of all Celtic fans of a certain age. But, sadly for the Parkhead faithful, it was a spectacle they were to witness all too infrequently, as one of the greatest talents of the day was lost to the game, long before he fulfilled his undoubted potential.

There was no doubt that George Connelly had it all. A central defender with an eye for goal, he was seen as the ideal replacement for captain Billy McNeill, and a glittering future surely lay ahead. Hoops fans were given their first glimpse of his talents when, as a 15-year-old, he displayed nerves of steel to keep the ball in the air the entire way round the Parkhead pitch before a vital European Cup Winners' Cup clash against Dynamo Kiev in January 1966.

Connelly broke into the Celtic first team in 1968, and when he robbed John Greig on the edge of the Rangers box to fire home the third goal in the 4-0 Scottish Cup Final drubbing of Rangers the following April, he ensured his place in the hearts of all Bhoys' fans.

He was maturing as a ball-winning playmaker, with distribution to match that of master craftsman Bertie Auld, and Connelly's growing reputation was even further enhanced when he scored the only goal of the 1970 European Cup semi-final first leg victory over Leeds United at Elland Road, paving the way for Celtic's second European Cup Final against Feyenoord.

Some of his appearances symbolise the bad luck he had in his career—he played in the losing European Cup side of 1970, in two losing Scottish Cup teams and in four unsuccessful League Cup Finals.

Connelly, who won the first of two full international caps for Scotland in a World Cup qualifier against Czechoslovakia, was far from happy in the spotlight. Claiming he could no longer take the pressures associated with the job, he walked out of the club in November 1973. He was never the same player again, and shortly after his return to the ranks broke his ankle in a European Cup clash with Basle of Switzerland in March 1974 and again his faith in the sport was tested.

Connelly, who was Scotland's Player of the Year in 1973 and was also described as Scotland's Franz Beckenbauer, once confided to a friend that he would have preferred to have been a long-distance lorry driver rather than a footballer!

He left Celtic to play briefly for Falkirk, before a lack of fitness forced a parting of the ways. He was later reinstated as a junior player with Sauchie.

Though he is long retired, the fame of George Connelly's football skills still prompts articles in the press lamenting the loss to Scottish football of such a talent, and contrasting how he lives now to what might have been on the international football stage.

TOMMY COYNE

Born: Govan, 14 November 1962
Celtic career: 1989 to 1993
Appearances and goals:

League		FA Cup		Lg Cup		Europe	
A	G	A	G	A	G	A	G
105	43	16	8	6	1	5	0

Total appearances: 132
Total goals: 52
Honours: 22 Republic of Ireland caps

One of the most prolific marksmen of his generation, 'Der Bomber' had trials for Celtic, but was twice passed over before Billy McNeill brought him to Parkhead to cover for Frank McAvennie's anticipated return to London.

He first sprang to prominence with Clydebank, and, in his second season with the club, netted 19 goals in 38 games. He started the 1983-84 season with 10 goals in the opening 11 games, before being sold to Dundee United, then a rising force in Scottish football as part of the New Firm, for £60,000.

Though he scored a few goals in the UEFA Cup, he failed to reproduce his form in the domestic competitions, and halfway through the 1986-87 campaign he was transferred to city rivals Dundee. He soon rediscovered his shooting boots, and in 1987-88 was the top scorer in the Premier Division—netting 33 goals in 43 matches.

Sold to Celtic in March 1989, Coyne initially failed to reproduce his form and did not find the net for the remainder of that season. The next season was also hardly a success, although he did net a treble against Hearts. Coyne also scored the goal in February 1990 that put Rangers out of the fourth round of the Scottish Cup.

In 1990-91 he regained his previous form, with 18 goals in 26 games, and he finished the season as the club's top scorer. The following season he found the net 15 times, including a League Cup treble against Montrose when Gerry Creaney also hit a hat-trick. His form had led to him winning full international honours for Jack Charlton's Republic of Ireland, for which he qualified under the grandparent rule. He made a memorable debut, scoring in a 2-1 win over Switzerland in March 1992.

Despite his goalscoring record for the Hoops, Coyne was transferred to Tranmere Rovers. He was not long at Prenton Park when he sadly lost his wife Alison, and decided to return north of the border with Motherwell who paid £125,000 for his services. It was in his early days as a Motherwell player that he enjoyed his greatest moment as an international. Playing as a lone striker against the Italians in the 1994 World Cup Finals, it was his tireless running that paved the way for a much celebrated 1-0 victory.

Coyne was the Scottish Premier Division's top scorer in 1994-95, ending with 59 goals in 132 games before rejoining Dundee. Here he was loaned out to Falkirk before returning to his first club Clydebank as player-manager. He was sacked after six months as the club had entered administration, despite being near the top of Division Two. After leaving Clydebank, he joined Albion Rovers where he ended his playing career. He later coached junior club Bellshill Athletic to West Division One title in 2003-04, but a year later he was sacked!

JIM CRAIG

Born: Glasgow, 30 April 1943
Celtic career: 1965 to 1972
Appearances and goals:

League		FA Cup		Lg Cup		Europe	
A	G	A	G	A	G	A	G
147	1	23	0	30	4	31	1

Total appearances: 231

Total goals: 6

League Championships: 1965-66; 1966-67; 1967-68; 1968-69; 1969-70; 1970-71; 1971-72
Scottish Cup: 1966-67; 1968-69; 1970-71; 1971-72
League Cup: 1967-68; 1968-69; 1969-70
European Cup: 1966-67
Honours: 1 Scotland cap

Jim Craig is probably the only Lisbon Lion to don the hoops part-time. The full-back was almost as well-known for his dental studies as his football career, which won him more medals than most, including a European Cup badge. He combined his University studies with a footballer's life until the summer of 1966, and became a first team regular at Parkhead soon after.

He had proved himself an outstanding athlete, and, while at university, came second by inches in the Long Jump against Lyn Davies, who went on to take the gold medal in the Tokyo Olympics of 1964.

Jim Craig took over from the injured Ian Young at Muirton in November

1965. After a solid performance, he held his place and made his European debut in the Cup Winners' Cup against Kiev in Tbilisi, where his lack of experience saw him receive his marching orders. Though he lost his place to Young for that season's Scottish Cup Final against Rangers which ended all-square, he returned to the side for the replay which the Hoops lost 1-0.

It was midway through the 1966-67 season that Craig became Tommy Gemmell's full-back partner, and, in the European Cup Final against Inter Milan, it was Craig who cut the ball back for Gemmell to thunder home Celtic's equaliser.

He relished the big stage, and once admitted he needed pressure to make him play better. Craig was a hard tackler who could also use the ball well, but was, surprisingly, only capped once by Scotland, who weren't exactly blessed with an abundance of good right-backs at the time. Because of dentistry, Jim Craig's career with Celtic ended prematurely and he played the last of his 231 games in the Scottish Cup Final of 1972 when Hibernian were beaten 6-1. He intended to make his career doing extractions and fillings, but following a spell in South Africa with Hellenic FXC, he moved on to Sheffield Wednesday.

He played only two part-time seasons at Hillsborough before calling time on his playing career. A spell as Waterford's manager followed, but dentistry was always his preferred employment choice. After making a successful side career as a broadcaster and journalist, Craig became a dentist at a Glasgow health centre.

Only the great Danny McGrain could be classed as a better right-back than Jim Craig, who will rightly be remembered as a Celtic hero.

JOE CRAIG

Born: Bridge of Allan, 14 May 1954
Celtic career: 1976 to 1978
Appearances and goals:

League		FA Cup		Lg Cup		Europe	
A	G	A	G	A	G	A	G
55	22	7	7	6	4	4	4

Total appearances: 72
Total goals: 37
League Championships: 1976-77
Scottish Cup: 1976-77
Honours: 1 Scotland cap

Joe Craig was a motor mechanic in Bathgate, and though his skills were much admired by the Football League's top managers, notably Bill Shankly of Liverpool and Bill Nicholson of Spurs, it was Partick Thistle boss Bertie Auld who persuaded him to join the Jags. His impressive displays for the

Firhill club led to him winning his first representative honours when he turned out for the Scottish League XI.

In September 1976, Celtic manager Jock Stein signed Craig as a replacement for Dixie Deans. An old-fashioned centre-forward with height and strength to lead the line, there is no doubt that his best season at Parkhead was his first, when Celtic won the League and Scottish Cup double.

Craig was in outstanding form, netting 34 goals in the League and playing in the triumphant Hoops side against Rangers in that season's Scottish Cup Final. Celtic finished nine points ahead of the Gers that season, and no matter who they played, Craig refused to show opposition defences any mercy!

His form for the Hoops led to him winning full international recognition for Scotland against Sweden in April 1977. Coming off the bench to replace Kenny Burns, he became the only Scottish player to score a goal before he'd kicked the ball—Craig's first touch was a header as Scotland beat the Swedes 3-1!

The scorer of some spectacular goals, Craig seemed to go off the boil after his successful 1976-77 campaign—due in the main to the departure of his goal-maker Kenny Dalglish—and he was eventually allowed to leave Parkhead and try his luck in the Football League with Blackburn Rovers.

Though he wasn't as prolific at Ewood Park, netting just eight goals in his 48 appearances for the Lancashire club, he did help Rovers win promotion to the Second Division before returning north of the Border to continue his career with Hamilton Academical. Unfortunately for both club and player, he spent most of his time with the Accies on the treatment table, and in 1983 the popular striker was forced to retire.

After being appointed coach at Cowdenbeath, Craig became the club's manager, but lost his job at Central Park as the result of a boardroom coup. In consequence, almost all of his 18 players voted to boycott pre-season training!

PAT CRERAND

Born: Glasgow, 19 February 1939
Celtic career: 1958 to 1963
Appearances and goals:

League		FA Cup		Lg Cup		Europe	
A	G	A	G	A	G	A	G
91	5	14	1	13	1	2	1

Total appearances: 120
Total goals: 8
Honours: 16 Scotland caps

An attacking right-half and one of Celtic's most popular players, Pat Crerand, despite his lack of genuine pace, loved to attack. His speciality was the long defence-splitting pass and a willingness to shoot. He provided some steel in the Hoops' midfield during the prolonged 'youth policy' practised by the club.

Though his period at Parkhead was barren of major domestic trophies, Crerand won seven of his 16 international caps for Scotland, represented the Scottish League on seven occasions and played for Celtic in the 1961 Scottish Cup Final, which the Hoops lost 2-0 to Dunfermline Athletic after a replay.

Pat Crerand's aggression also got him into trouble on the field. He had been ordered off twice: playing for Scotland against Czechoslovakia and during a five-a-side tournament in Falkirk, both in 1961. Such indiscipline meant that he would fall foul of Celtic's chairman Bob Kelly. The SFA suspended him for seven days for the sending-off in Europe, but Celtic sidelined him for a month—and on half-wages—since Kelly felt that his offences reflected badly on the Parkhead club's image.

Things came to a head after the 1963 Ne'erday game at Ibrox against Rangers, when a flare-up with coach Sean Fallon resulted in Crerand's name never again featuring on a Celtic team sheet.

The following month, on the recommendation of Manchester United star Denis Law, Crerand joined the Old Trafford club for a fee of £56,000—at the time a record transfer fee for a wing-half. After only a few months with the club, he won an FA Cup winners' medal as the Reds beat Leicester City 3-1.

A thoughtful player with a firm belief in attacking, constructive football, the former Celtic player initiated numerous attacks for the Red Devils with long, shrewd passes. He soon began to give United a much more balanced look—he was an architect, sweeping out accurate crossfield passes of 40 and 50 yards to his forwards.

Along with England stars Bobby Charlton and Nobby Stiles, he formed the midfield trio that drove Manchester United to victory in the European Cup. He also went on to win two League Championship medals, his creative skills being a big factor in the club's success throughout the 1960s. After United's 4-3 win against Manchester City at Maine Road on the final day of the 1970-71 season, Crerand decided to retire, having played in 392 first team games for the Old Trafford club.

He subsequently became coach and assistant-manager at United, and though in 1976 the Hoops wanted a new assistant to Jock Stein, the Reds boss Tommy Docherty would not endorse Crerand as a candidate. He was manager of Northampton Town from the summer of 1976 to January 1977, but on ending his involvement with the game, became a PR officer for a Manchester engineering company and a pub landlord at the Park Hotel in Altrincham.

KENNY DALGLISH

Born: Glasgow, 4 March 1951
Celtic career: 1970 to 1977
Appearances and goals:

League		FA Cup		Lg Cup		Europe	
A	**G**	**A**	**G**	**A**	**G**	**A**	**G**
200/4	112	30	11	56/3	35	27/1	9

Total appearances: 313/8
Total goals: 167
League Championships: 1971-72; 1972-73; 1973-74; 1976-77
Scottish Cup: 1971-72; 1973-74; 1974-75; 1976-77
League Cup: 1974-75
Honours: 102 Scotland caps

Sean Fallon's power of persuasion was severely tested before he left the Dalglish home in the south side of Glasgow with the signature of a young man who was to become one of the greatest Celtic players of all time. Hearing that Fallon was at the door, Dalglish raced to his bedroom and frantically tore down the posters of his boyhood Rangers idols! The legendary first meeting between Jock Stein's assistant and Dalglish is etched in Celtic folklore—leaving his wife waiting in the car outside for 'a wee minute'— Fallon returned some two-and-a-half hours later with the lifelong Rangers fan's signature.

He joined Celtic in 1967 as a 16-year-old and was farmed out to Cumbernauld United, for whom he scored 37 goals during the 1967-68 season. He also worked as an apprentice joiner. By the following year he had turned professional and was a regular member of the Celtic reserve team, who were so good they were known as the Quality Street Gang.

Dalglish made his debut from the bench in a Scottish League Cup quarter-final tie at Hamilton Academical at Douglas Park in September 1968, helping the Hoops to a 4-2 victory. It took him three years to establish himself in the first team, for at that time Celtic were not only the best team in Scotland but had just become the first British team to win the European Cup. Stein took a great interest in Dalglish, recognising his potentially outstanding talent. Eventually he gave him his chance in a benefit match—the result was that Dalglish scored six of Celtic's goals in a 7-2 defeat of Kilmarnock!

The 1971-72 season saw Dalglish score his first goal for Celtic—it came via the penalty-spot in the 2-0 League Cup tie win over childhood favourites Rangers at Ibrox—and he went on to amass 23 League and Cup goals in just 49 appearances by the end of the season. By 1972-73, Dalglish was Celtic's leading marksman with a seasonal tally of 41 goals in all competitions. Dalglish was made Celtic captain in 1975-76, but it was a miserable year. Stein was badly hurt in a car crash and missed most of the season, and Celtic failed to win a trophy for the first time in 12 years.

Kenny Dalglish (www.snspix.com)

A central figure in the Scottish sides which went to the 1974 and 1978 World Cup Finals, Dalglish was Scotland's most capped player, and was a sound enough finisher to share the Scottish international scoring record of 30 with Denis Law. In 1976 he scored the winning goal for Scotland against England at Hampden Park when he put the ball through Ray Clemence's legs. A year later he scored against the same opponents and goalkeeper at Wembley in another 2-1 win.

Though he scored 167 goals in 321 appearances, Dalglish was never regarded as an out-and-out striker. He was often used by Jock Stein as a link-man just behind the lethal pairing of 'Dixie' Deans and Bobby Lennox.

In August 1977, Dalglish moved to Bob Paisley's Liverpool for a then-record £440,000 transfer fee—bought as a replacement for Kevin Keegan, who had joined Hamburg SV. He ended his first season at Anfield as top scorer as Liverpool stormed to the League title, and Dalglish was voted Footballer of the Year. After joining the Reds, he made 177 consecutive League and Cup appearances before missing his first game in 1980. That was the year he picked up another European Cup winners' medal and Liverpool retained their League title.

He had been instrumental in Liverpool winning the 1978 European Cup Final against Bruges, scoring the only goal of the game. The Merseyside outfit continued to dominate British football, and, in 1983, he scored his 100th goal for the Reds to become only the third player ever to score a century of goals in both Scottish and English football. He was voted Footballer of the Year again, and picked up the players' Player of the Year award as Liverpool celebrated their 14th Championship.

Following the Heysel Stadium disaster, Dalglish was appointed player-manager. His first season in charge could not have been more successful, as the Reds completed the League and FA Cup double. However, in February 1991, Dalglish rocked the football world by resigning, citing the pressures of the job.

Suitably refreshed after a few months out, he returned to management in October of that year with Blackburn Rovers, leading the club to the Premiership via the play-offs. In 1994-95 Rovers won the Premier League title. He later stepped down to become Director of Football, but then announced his departure from Ewood Park. After a spell in charge at Newcastle United, he returned to Parkhead as Director of Football operations, but left the club following the appointment of Martin O'Neill.

DIXIE DEANS

Born: Linwood, 30 July 1946
Celtic career: 1971 to 1976
Appearances and goals:

League		FA Cup		Lg Cup		Europe	
A	G	A	G	A	G	A	G
122/4	89	21	18	21/1	11	11/3	6

Total appearances: 175/8
Total goals: 124
League Championships: 1971-72; 1972-73; 1973-74
Scottish Cup: 1971-72; 1973-74
League Cup: 1974-75
Honours: 2 Scotland caps

Nicknamed after the pre-war Everton and England centre-forward Dixie Dean, he made an immediate impact with Celtic after signing from Motherwell in October 1971 for a bargain £17,500. The short and stocky Motherwell striker had a chronic history of trouble on the field, and was serving a six-week suspension when he put pen to paper!

Deans first came to prominence as a prolific scorer with Neilston, and when he netted a staggering 60 goals in one season, Motherwell pipped Newcastle United for his signature. In only his second season at Fir Park, he broke the club's post-war goalscoring record by netting 30 League goals—his exploits paving the way for promotion. However, during his time with the Steelmen, controversy continually clouded his career. Not long after scoring a hat-trick against Dunfermline Athletic, he was sent off in the match against Celtic in December 1966. There followed a number of other dismissals, and, at one stage, Deans threatened to end his career and emigrate.

He enjoyed a prolific career with the Hoops, especially when Hibernian were the opposition! He netted a hat-trick in the 6-1 defeat of the Edinburgh club in the 1972 Scottish Cup Final, and against the same opposition in a 6-3 League Cup Final victory in the 1974-75 competition. In fact in 13 matches against the Easter Road club, he scored an astonishing 18 goals. Sandwiched in between these two outstanding achievements was the 7-0 home win over Partick Thistle in November 1973, when Deans hit the target an incredible six times!

Just before his hat-trick against Hibs in the 1972 Scottish Cup Final, Deans experienced his worst moment in football—when he missed his penalty in the shoot-out after extra-time at Celtic Park against Inter Milan, costing Celtic a place in the European Cup Final.

Deans, who had a great rapport with Celtic fans, who liked his wholehearted style, won every domestic honour in the game while with the Hoops, and was twice capped by Scotland against East Germany and Spain.

In the summer of 1976 he was transferred to Luton Town for £20,000, but his stay at Kenilworth Road was brief and, after a loan spell with Carlisle United, he joined Partick Thistle on trial. He later went to Australia to play for Adelaide City, and is still a hero to the Adelaide fans for his goalscoring exploits when he was the leading scorer in Australia in 1977-78. Deans later wound down his playing career in Ireland with Shelbourne.

Dixie is a match-day host at Parkhead, where along with other Celtic legends he entertains corporate facility guests. He also has business interests in Glasgow, owning 'Dixie's' pub in Rutherglen as well as being involved with former Hoops player Tommy Callaghan in the firm Esperanza Property Development, a company that buys, renovates and sells properties throughout Central Scotland.

PAOLO DI CANIO

Born: Rome, 9 July 1968
Celtic career: 1996 to 1997
Appearances and goals:

League		FA Cup		Lg Cup		Europe	
A	**G**	**A**	**G**	**A**	**G**	**A**	**G**
25/1	12	6	3	2	0	2/1	0

Total appearances: 35/2
Total goals: 15

There is no doubt that Celtic manager Tommy Burns knew he was taking a chance when he brought volatile Italian maestro Paolo Di Canio to Scotland from Serie A giants AC Milan in the summer of 1996.

Di Canio had played for four of his country's biggest clubs in Lazio, Juventus, Napoli and AC Milan, before arriving at Parkhead and making his League debut against Raith Rovers. The Celtic faithful did not have long to wait before sampling the two sides of the character who was both to thrill and infuriate them in the season that lay ahead. Delightful touches of skill, seldom seen from any other Hoops player since the heady days of the late 1960s and early 1970s, were interspersed with bouts of petulance which he clearly believed would endear him to the home supporters.

The gamble paid off in a big way, and he immediately became a hero of the Green and White Army who recognised that, if his temperament could be harnessed by Burns, he might just be the player to bring the glory days back to Parkhead.

Di Canio took to life in Glasgow like a duck to water, and his off-field contentment was mirrored on the park with a string of breathtaking displays which had journalists struggling to find new superlatives. But as with all geniuses, the magic came at a price. Di Canio's short temper found him constantly in hot water with the match officials, but the two red cards, along with countless yellows he received, only served to heighten his appeal with the Hoops' fans.

The players' Player of the Year award was testament to the regard in which he was held by his peers, but an end-of-season bust up with chairman Fergus McCann—which resulted in the Italian being fined two weeks' wages—coupled with his failure to turn up for pre-season training, cast a huge shadow over his future with the club, and shortly afterwards he moved into the Premiership with Sheffield Wednesday.

He was the Owls' leading scorer in 1997-98, but is famous for an incident on the pitch where he pushed referee Paul Alcock to the ground after being sent off playing against Arsenal. In January 1999, Di Canio signed for West Ham United and helped them to achieve a high league position and qualify for the UEFA Cup, albeit through the 'back door' route of the Intertoto Cup. He scored the BBC Goal of the Season in 2000 with a volley against Wimbledon—a strike which is still considered among the best goals in Premiership history.

In 2001 he won the FIFA Fair Play award after shunning a goal-scoring opportunity against Everton, catching the ball while the Everton keeper Paul Gerrard was lying injured on the ground. He remained at Upton Park until 2003 when, following a very public row with Glenn Roeder following the Hammers' relegation, he signed for Charlton Athletic.

In August 2004, Di Canio, who had a chequered career, moved back to his home-team Lazio having already signed an extension to his Charlton contract, which involved taking a massive pay cut. He played for two seasons with Lazio before leaving to join Cisco Roma of Serie C2 on a free transfer.

SIMON DONNELLY

Born: Glasgow, 1 December 1974
Celtic career: 1993 to 1999
Appearances and goals:

League		FA Cup		Lg Cup		Europe	
A	G	A	G	A	G	A	G
113/33	30	8/5	2	11/6	4	13/7	6

Total appearances: 145/51
Total goals: 42
League Championships: 1997-98
Scottish Cup: 1994-95
League Cup: 1997-98
Honours: 10 Scotland caps

The son of Tom Donnelly who played for both Rangers and Motherwell,

Simon started his career with Queen's Park before switching to Celtic in 1993.

After making his Hoops' debut as a substitute in the goalless draw at Hibernian in March 1994, Donnelly became an integral member of the Celtic side for the next four seasons. He won his first piece of silverware as Celtic beat Airdrie 1-0 to win the 1995 Scottish Cup Final, and his form over the next couple of seasons led to him winning full international honours for Scotland.

In fact, the first nine of Simon Donnelly's 10 appearances for his country involved him coming off the bench, and it was only on his last appearance, against the Faroe Islands in October 1998, that he started the game.

Forming a quite formidable strike force with Sweden's Henrik Larsson, Donnelly had his best season with the club in 1997-98, scoring 10 goals in 21 starts, including a brace in the 4-1 defeat of Motherwell. He also netted Celtic's goals in the 1-1 draw at Dunfermline Athletic in the penultimate game of the campaign. The Hoops went on to win the League Championship by two points from runners-up Rangers.

That season, Donnelly suffered a number of niggling injuries and had to be content with a place on the bench for the League Cup Final against Dundee United. Replacing Thom, he played his part in the club's 3-0 success.

In the summer of 1999, Donnelly, along with Celtic team-mate Phil O'Donnell, controversially left Parkhead and joined Sheffield Wednesday on a Bosman free transfer. Although he made the starting line-up for the opening game of the 1999-2000 season against Liverpool, he suffered a very frustrating campaign thanks to a string of injury problems. He was then dogged by hamstring problems, although he did return to score a marvellous winner in the Yorkshire derby against Barnsley. Injury problems continued to hamper his progress, and with Wednesday slipping down the leagues to what was the Second Division, Donnelly opted for a move back to Scotland.

He spent a season playing for St Johnstone before being signed by Davie Hay at Dunfermline Athletic. However, the unlucky Donnelly suffered from yet more injuries, and after a couple of seasons with the Pars, he was released.

In the summer of 2006, Donnelly moved on to Scottish First Division club Partick Thistle on a two-year deal.

ROBERT DOUGLAS

Born: Lanark, 24 April 1972
Celtic career: 2000 to 2005
Appearances and goals:

League		FA Cup		Lg Cup		Europe	
A	**G**	**A**	**G**	**A**	**G**	**A**	**G**
107/1	0	17	0	7	0	30	0

Total appearances: 161/1
Total goals: 0
League Championships: 2000-01; 2001-02; 2003-04
Scottish Cup: 2000-01; 2003-04; 2004-05
Honours: 19 Scotland caps

Despite a number of Celtic fans labelling him 'Butterfingers Douglas', he made over 100 League appearances and was a key part of the team that reached the 2002-03 UEFA Cup Final.

A former brickie, Douglas played his early football for Livingston, helping his team win the Third Division Championship, before joining Dundee in the summer of 1997. An ever-present in his first season at Dens Park, he helped the Dark Blues win the First Division Championship, keeping 17 clean sheets. In fact, Douglas had played 348 minutes of first team football for Dundee before he conceded his first goal! His performances eventually led to him moving to Celtic in October 2000 for a fee of £1.2 million.

Though Martin O'Neill had to beat off competition from Rangers' Dick Advocaat to sign the impressively-built keeper, it took Douglas a while to become accustomed to the pressures of playing football for a club of Celtic's stature. Following an Old Firm debut disaster a month after putting pen to paper, when the Light Blues beat Celtic 5-1, Douglas struggled to win over many Hoops' fans, but he did play his part in the club winning the SPL Championship and kept a clean sheet in the Scottish Cup Final as Celtic beat Hibernian 3-0.

The following season, Douglas won full international honours for Scotland, this after he had confounded his critics with some exceptional performances, especially in the Champions League qualifiers against Ajax. In 2002-03, Douglas was outstanding in the club's run to the UEFA Cup Final, where they were beaten 3-2 after extra time by Porto. It was a season in which Celtic were also runners-up to Rangers in both the League and League Cup.

Though there were occasions when he seemed to lack authority—especially on crosses—Rob Douglas' shot-stopping ability was second to none. One of the best Celtic keepers since Packie Bonner, it seemed he would have a lengthy Parkhead and international career ahead of him, but, after a 6-0 loss to Holland in Amsterdam in a 2003 play-off qualification to the Euro 2004

Rob Douglas

competition, for which he was largely blamed, he lost his position as the nation's first-choice keeper.

During the 2004-05 season, he faced stiff competition from youngster David Marshall, and, at the end of the campaign, he was told by O'Neill that he wouldn't be the club's first-choice custodian the following season. Douglas then decided that he wanted to test himself in England rather than sit on the bench, and joined Leicester City on a free transfer. Despite injuring himself at home in a freak accident—when he slipped on the stairs—he remained between the posts until being replaced towards the end of the campaign by Paul Henderson and former youth academy keeper Conrad Logan.

JOHNNY DOYLE

Born: Uddingston, 11 May 1951
Died: 19 October 1981
Celtic career: 1976 to 1981
Appearances and goals:

League		FA Cup		Lg Cup		Europe	
A	**G**	**A**	**G**	**A**	**G**	**A**	**G**
104/14	15	16/2	7	29/5	14	8/3	1

Total appearances: 157/24
Total goals: 37
League Championships: 1976-77; 1978-79; 1980-81
Scottish Cup: 1976-77; 1979-80
Honours: 1 Scotland cap

Ironically, it was Johnny Doyle's dismissal while playing for Ayr United against his boyhood heroes Celtic that brought about him joining the Parkhead club. Doyle had been suspended by the SFA as a result of this misdemeanour, and shortly afterwards, in an interview with a reporter, said he was 'fed up of being kicked about for £30 a week. I want to go to Celtic'. A week later, on 15 March 1976, he joined the Hoops for a fee of £90,000.

Having joined Ayr United from Viewpark FC in the summer of 1970, Doyle soon demonstrated his ability to play on either flank, and his early form earned him selection for Scotland's Under-23 side. Noted for his exceptional speed, full international honours followed in December 1975 when he played against Romania at Hampden. In fact, it was Doyle's cross that was converted by the unmarked Bruce Rioch to earn Scotland a 1-1 draw.

After overcoming an injury on his debut for the Hoops at Dundee, he soon became a great favourite with the Celtic fans. In fact, some of the Parkhead club's greatest moments were the work of the speedy Doyle. In the Scottish Cup competition of 1979-80 in a packed Love Street, he netted a superb solo goal against St Mirren. Picking up the ball deep in his own half, he ran through the entire defence before scoring from a virtually impossible angle. A fortnight later, the whole of Parkhead erupted when he squeezed between two Real Madrid defenders to send home an amazing header to put the Hoops 2-0 up in the European Cup quarter-final first leg.

However, when the Hoops won the League Championship against Rangers at Parkhead the previous season, he received his marching orders. Celtic won the title with 10 men, because, in a moment of madness early in the second half, Johnny Doyle kicked Alex Macdonald as he was lying prone with the Light Blues leading 1-0. Stunned with remorse, he could barely be persuaded to join in the after-match celebrations!

Though he could be inconsistent, Johnny Doyle was a virtual ever-present in the Celtic team until the arrival of Davie Provan, and, when at the top of his game, was capable of destroying the most resolute of defences.

Sadly, the flying winger died from electrocution, aged only 30, while working in the loft of his new home in Kilmarnock in October 1981. Celtic played Ipswich Town at Portman Road the following month, and the club's fans staged a spontaneous two minutes silence for Johnny Doyle in the centre of the Suffolk town.

BOBBY EVANS

Born: Glasgow, 16 July 1927
Died: Airdrie, 1 September 2001
Celtic career: 1944 to 1960
Appearances and goals:

League		FA Cup		Lg Cup		Europe	
A	**G**	**A**	**G**	**A**	**G**	**A**	**G**
385	10	64	0	88	1	-	-

Total appearances: 537
Total goals: 11
League Championships: 1953-54
Scottish Cup: 1950-51; 1953-54
League Cup: 1956-57; 1957-58
Honours: 48 Scotland caps

Signed from St Anthony's in 1944, Bobby Evans was the original model of the now-fashionable wing-back. The powerful little redhead was the type of player which every manager wanted in his side. Strong, with energy to burn, Evans was perfect for the role—keen but scrupulously fair in the tackle, powerful in the air, a wonderful reader of the game and with the enthusiasm of a youngster.

An apprentice joiner, Evans made his Celtic debut as an inside-forward in an unofficial wartime fixture against Albion Rovers, but had to wait until the final game of the 1947-48 season before making his League debut against Dundee. Within a few months of breaking into the first team, Evans had made his mark on the international scene. Following a victorious debut against Wales in Cardiff, he inspired his country to a thrilling 3-2 win over Ireland after being two goals down at Hampden in 1948.

Celtic's long-awaited Scottish Cup victory of 1950-51 and the historic St Mungo Cup win of the same season gave Evans his first taste of major success. He then went on to give the sustained performance of a lifetime throughout the unexpectedly triumphant Coronation Cup run two years later. In the final, Evans was regarded by many as simply sublime as he played the great Lawrie Reilly out of the game and fittingly instigated the move that led to Jimmy Walsh's clinching strike in the 2-0 defeat of favourites Hibernian.

Celtic won the League and Cup double in 1953-54—their first for 40 years—with Evans demonstrating his stamina, determination and sheer will to win. He was the first Celtic captain to lift the League Cup in 1956 as the Hoops beat Partick Thistle, and he famously helped defend it a year later as Celtic thrashed Rangers 7-1.

Towards the end of his international career, Evans took over the captaincy of Scotland—a job he retained with supreme confidence. He moved to a central defensive berth late in his Parkhead career, but even with Billy McNeill in the wings, fans were shocked when, in May 1960, Evans was suddenly transferred to Chelsea for a fee of £12,000.

After his Celtic days, however, his career went into decline. Moves to Newport County (as player-manager), Morton, Third Lanark and Raith Rovers were relatively unsuccessful, though he did play his part in the latter club's return to the First Division in 1967.

Nicknamed 'Dai' because of his Welsh surname, Bobby Evans will always be remembered as a Celtic legend. At his best, he was a magnificent and courageous player for the club in a career which spanned over 500 games in the green and white.

SEAN FALLON

Born: Sligo, Ireland, 31 July 1922
Celtic career: 1950 to 1958
Appearances and goals:

League		FA Cup		Lg Cup		Europe	
A	G	A	G	A	G	A	G
178	8	31	2	47	3	-	-

Total appearances: 256
Total goals: 13
League Championships: 1953-54
Scottish Cup: 1950-51; 1953-54
League Cup: 1956-57; 1957-58
Honours: 8 Republic of Ireland caps

Though Sean Fallon's name is synonymous with Celtic, the 'Iron Man' played his early football with St Mary's Juniors and also played Gaelic football for Craobh Ruadh. He also played for McArthurs, Sligo Distillery and Longford Town before he arrived at the Showgrounds in 1947 to play for Sligo Rovers. He then joined Glenavon in the north before impressing the Hoops with his performance for the Irish League against the League of Ireland.

Sean Fallon's love affair with Celtic started when the son of the Celtic legend Jimmy McMenemy saved Fallon's sister Lily from drowning at Lough Gill. Fallon invited Joe McMenemy back to his house, and the Scot returned the compliment by sending Sean presents of a Celtic shirt and Willy Maley's book *The Story of the Celtic*. He realised his ambition when

Sean Fallon, left, in 1973, when acting as assistant to the Big Man himself, Jock Stein (www.snspix.com)

he made his league debut for Celtic, away to Clyde in the last game of the 1949-50 season, though he did score an own goal in a 2-2 draw!

Within a year, he had helped the Hoops win the Scottish Cup, beating Motherwell 1-0 in the final. Fallon said later, 'As I walked off Hampden I felt I had got everything out of life I had ever wanted. I had become a member of the famous Celtic FC and holder of a Scottish Cup badge all in one year.' Two years later, he would also have a Cup Final goal to celebrate as he scored in the Scottish Cup Final as Celtic went on to defeat Aberdeen.

After making his full international debut for the Republic of Ireland against Norway in November 1950, he went on to win eight caps, five at full-back and three in the No.9 shirt. As a centre-forward, he went against the French 'like a battering ram' and scored after 20 minutes in a 1-1 draw, He also found the net in his final game for his country against West Germany in November 1955.

Celtic rewarded his wholehearted endeavour with the club captaincy. His left arm was chronically susceptible to cracks and breaks, and he had to surrender the skipper's role most of the time to his deputy Jock Stein. A broken collarbone against Hearts in October 1953 kept him out for much of the 1953-54 double-winning season. He went off in the 65th minute, but then returned with his arm in a sling to play out the match at outside-left!

Fallon was back to full fitness for another momentous occasion in Celtic's history—the League Cup Final victory in 1957, when Celtic beat Rangers 7-1 at Hampden Park, the so-called 'Hampden in the Sun' game.

He was forced to retire in 1958 through a knee injury, but his influence and importance to the club continued. He became assistant to Jock Stein when Stein took up the post of manager in 1965. When Jock Stein survived a near-fatal car crash in 1975, Fallon took over as caretaker manager.

He was an integral part of Celtic's success under Jock Stein, when he was the manager's right-hand man, and his powers of persuasion were often called upon to secure the signatures of promising young players who would go on to become Celtic legends—Tommy Gemmell, Lou Macari, David Hay, Danny McGrain, Kenny Dalglish and Packie Bonner!

He left Glasgow to become assistant-manager at Dumbarton in 1978, later taking over the reins before, in 1986, becoming a director at Clyde. Fiercely proud of his connections with Celtic, Sean Fallon was awarded a testimonial dinner by the Parkhead club in October 1993, and once assessed his own talents as a player by saying 'I was just an ordinary player with a big heart and a fighting spirit to recommend me.'

WILLIE FERNIE

Born: Kinglassie, 22 November 1928
Celtic career: 1948 to 1958 and 1960 to 1961
Appearances and goals:

League		FA Cup		Lg Cup		Europe	
A	**G**	**A**	**G**	**A**	**G**	**A**	**G**
219	55	39	10	59	11	-	-

Total appearances: 317
Total goals: 76
League Championships: 1953-54
Scottish Cup: 1953-54
League Cup: 1956-57; 1957-58
Honours: 12 Scotland caps

A masterly and mesmeric dribbler, Willie Fernie began his career with Leslie Hearts and appeared in the 1948 Scottish Juvenile Cup Final at Easter

Road, before later signing for Celtic. During his early days at Parkhead, Fernie was farmed out to the local side Kinglassie Colliery.

Having made his Celtic debut in a 1-0 win at St Mirren in March 1950, Fernie soon established himself at inside-right, although there were occasions when he appeared as a winger. Celtic's journey through the 1950s was an erratic one—they beat Motherwell 1-0 to win the 1951 Scottish Cup, yet were eliminated in the first round stage the following year. He had a tremendous Coronation Cup campaign in 1953, and his performance in the final victory over Hibernian prompted Charlie Tully to say 'If Willie had a left foot, we'd have won the game at half-time!'

The double won in 1953-54—the club's first for 40 years—saw Willie Fernie's dribble and cross for Sean Fallon to score, which brought the Scottish Cup home in the process. The decade also contained the result that has always acted as a source of provocation to Rangers' supporters, when Celtic claimed the League Cup at Hampden—Fernie, who was the most influential figure on the field, netting a last minute penalty in a 7-1 win for Celtic!

In December 1958, Fernie was transferred to Middlesbrough for £17,500—the fee matching the Teesside club's record transfer, paid to take Bill Harris to Ayresome Park from Hull City four years earlier. It was here that he came into contact with the young Brian Clough, but never in his 22-month stay did the two players see eye-to-eye.

Fernie then returned to Parkhead for a reported £12,000, and scored in his last match against Rangers at Ibrox in September 1961 before opting for a move to St Mirren. While at Love Street, he gained a second successive Scottish Cup runners-up medal in 1962. Fernie, who won all the domestic honours with Celtic, was capped 12 times by Scotland, appearing in both the 1954 and 1958 World Cup Finals. He also represented the Scottish League XI on four occasions.

After spells at Alloa and in Ireland with Bangor, Fernie subsequently returned to Parkhead as the club's youth coach, before in October 1973 joining Kilmarnock as manager. He led Killie to promotion back to Division One in his first season with the club, and then, after league reconstruction, to promotion to the new Premier Division in 1975-76. However, Killie struggled in the top flight, and were unsurprisingly relegated in 1976-77. A bad start to the following season saw him sacked and resolving to leave the football industry.

Latterly, he has run a small taxi-cab business in the Castlemilk district of Glasgow.

MIKE GALLOWAY

Born: Oswestry, 30 May 1965
Celtic career: 1989 to 1995
Appearances and goals:

League		FA Cup		Lg Cup		Europe	
A	**G**	**A**	**G**	**A**	**G**	**A**	**G**
103/22	8	7/4	0	13/2	0	9	2

Total appearances: 132/28
Total goals: 10
Honours: 1 Scotland cap

Mike Galloway trained for eight weeks at Ibrox until Davie Provan told him the Light Blues weren't interested. Then, at Leicester City, the Foxes manager Jock Wallace turned him down on the grounds of size. But finally, Berwick Rangers boss Frank Connor signed him and he proceeded to give a series of polished displays, primarily as a defensive midfielder.

His performances led to him joining Mansfield Town, where he also played as a full-back and as a striker. In fact, he did so well at Field Mill, that Halifax town manager Mick Jones undertook sponsored walks to raise the transfer fee to take Galloway to The Shay.

At Halifax, he was used as a centre-half, and though he was watched on a number of occasions by Rangers manager Graeme Souness, Hearts astonished the football world by securing his services for £60,000. Quickly earning a reputation as a hard tackler, Galloway was played up front with great success by Hearts in their European campaign of 1988-89, so that when Celtic came in for him in the summer of 1989, it took £500,000 to prise him from the Edinburgh club.

Galloway's early form at Parkhead was outstanding, and led to him winning a couple of Scottish Under-21 caps as an over-age player in 1989-90, qualifying as the son of a Scottish soldier. He was elevated to senior status in October 1991 when Scotland played Romania in Bucharest.

At club level he featured as a substitute in Celtic's 1990 Scottish Cup Final defeat (on penalties) by Aberdeen and then was in the club's starting line-up for the 1994-95 League Cup Final against Raith Rovers, again lost on penalties. In between these two reversals, he gave away the embarrassing goal that sent rivals Rangers into the final of the League Cup at Ibrox in September 1993.

After various fines for breaches of club discipline, Mike Galloway joined Leicester City on loan in January 1995. However, he injured a hamstring during his first training session and the loan was postponed pending his fitness. Impressing with his strength and energetic commitment, he again suffered injury, but despite a further loan spell, the Foxes didn't want a permanent deal, and Galloway returned to Parkhead.

Sadly, his career was cut short by a terrible road accident in 1995 which shattered his pelvis and legs. Although he was given a £200,000 testimonial by Celtic the following year, Galloway has since suffered a history of drink and depression-related problems.

TOMMY GEMMELL

Born: Motherwell, 16 October 1943
Celtic career: 1961 to 1971
Appearances and goals:

League		FA Cup		Lg Cup		Europe	
A	G	A	G	A	G	A	G
247	38	43	4	74	10	51	11

Total appearances: 415
Total goals: 63
League Championships: 1965-66; 1966-67; 1967-68; 1968-69; 1969-70; 1970-71
Scottish Cup: 1964-65; 1966-67; 1968-69
League Cup: 1965-66; 1966-67; 1967-68; 1968-69;
European Cup: 1966-67
Honours: 18 Scotland caps

Tommy Gemmell was without doubt one of the best defenders ever to wear the distinctive hoops of Celtic, but first and foremost he was an entertainer. A flamboyant full-back with a thunderous shot in either foot, 'Big Tam' was idolised by the Parkhead faithful... and he knew it!

People will always remember his unstoppable drive that guided the Hoops to victory in the European Cup Final in 1967. He repeated the feat three years later in another European Cup Final against Feyenoord of Holland in the San Siro Stadium, but this time there was to be no happy ending. The Dutch side came back to equalise and then snatch the trophy in extra time with a goal from Ove Kindval. Gemmell was also on target in the 1968 World Club Championship against the notorious Racing Club of Buenos Aires, when he netted from the penalty spot. You could say he was a man for the big occasion.

He joined Celtic from Coltness United in the summer of 1961, and got the nickname 'Danny Kaye' because of his resemblance to the American comedian.

A tremendous long-range shot helped Gemmell score 63 goals in 415 appearances. A remarkable 31 of them came from penalties, a task Big Tam relished. 'Just make sure you keep it under the crossbar' was a philosophy which paid off for him all but three times in ten years. Jock Stein once tried Gemmell at centre-forward in a tour of America in 1966. He promptly rattled in a hat-trick, prompting Stein to say, 'You're wasted at centre-forward... you would have got at least four from left-back.'

Tommy Gemmell in action for Celtic in 1966 (www.snspix.com)

However, Tommy Gemmell did not always see eye to eye with Jock Stein, but neither man allowed this to interfere with the business of filling the Parkhead trophy room. By his own admission, though, Gemmell risked the 'rollicking of my life' when he followed fellow full-back Jim Craig upfield, in the move that led to his unforgettable goal in the 1967 European Cup Final victory over Inter Milan.

Capped 18 times by Scotland, the big defender holds a couple of unwanted distinctions—an own goal that sailed over the head of Ronnie Simpson to put the USSR into the lead in May 1967, and then, when playing against Germany in Hamburg in May 1969, he took a flying kick at Haller in retaliation near the end of the game and was sent off! Following this dismissal, Celtic disciplined him by giving Davie Hay the left-back spot for the League Cup Final against St Johnstone three days later.

In December 1971, Gemmell left Parkhead to join Nottingham Forest, for a fee of £40,000. A lawnmower accident during his time at the City ground seemed to damage his prospects in the Football League, and in July 1973 he returned to Scotland to play for Dundee, where he captained the club to a League Cup Final victory over Celtic in his first season.

He called time on his playing days at the end of the 1976-77 season to become Dundee's manager, a post he held until April 1980. He later ran a hotel in Perthshire and managed Albion Rovers. Now working for Sun Life Assurance, Tommy Gemmell, who a few years ago sold all his football medals at a Christie's auction in Glasgow, also entertains supporters as an after-dinner speaker.

RONNIE GLAVIN

Born: Glasgow, 27 March 1951
Celtic career: 1974 to 1979
Appearances and goals:

League		FA Cup		Lg Cup		Europe	
A	**G**	**A**	**G**	**A**	**G**	**A**	**G**
101	35	12	8	29	3	7	2

Total appearances: 149
Total goals: 48
League Championships: 1976-77; 1978-79
Scottish Cup: 1974-75
Honours: 1 Scotland cap

Having played his early football for Lochend Rovers, midfielder Ronnie Glavin joined Partick Thistle, and, while playing for their reserves, netted a quickfire hat-trick in a 4-1 defeat of Celtic. Within days he was in the Jags' senior side, and in October 1971, he helped Thistle beat Celtic by a similar scoreline to lift the League Cup.

Though Rangers' manager Willie Wallace was interested in taking Glavin to Ibrox, he was Roman Catholic, and so it was to Parkhead that he moved in November 1974.

He scored on his Hoops' debut in a 6-0 demolition of Airdrie, though until the arrival of Pat Stanton, much of his early time at Parkhead required him to do his fair share of marking. In 1976-77, in a free-running role as successor to Tommy Callaghan, he fed off the chances created by Joe Craig and Kenny Dalglish, and his goals went a long way towards helping the Hoops win the double, though he was missing from the Scottish Cup Final line up.

His absence was as a result of him winning his only full cap for the national side! Playing for Scotland against Sweden in April 1977, he was injured after only three minutes and replaced by Sandy Jardine, this causing him to miss the Scottish Cup Final against Rangers a fortnight later, a match the Hoops won 1-0.

Having scored 48 goals in 149 games, his performances for Celtic attracted interest from south of the Border, and in the summer of 1979 he was allowed to leave Parkhead and join Barnsley for a fee of £50,000.

He was hugely popular at Oakwell, where he spent five good seasons. Enjoying more of an attacking role, Glavin scored 73 goals in 176 games for the Tykes, with many of his strikes being spectacular long-range goals. His consistency in the middle of the park was a major factor in the Yorkshire club winning promotion to Division Two in 1980-81.

On leaving Barnsley, he joined Portuguese club Beleneuses on a free transfer, but later returned to Oakwell as the club's coach. A year later, in March 1986, Glavin left the club for a second time to become player-coach of Stockport County. While at Edgeley Park he had a brief spell as the club's caretaker-manager, but his time in charge was brief, and he returned north of the Border to play for Cowdenbeath on a match-to-match contract.

A few months later he left to play indoor football for his brother Tony's team, St Louis Steamers, in the United States.

JONATHAN GOULD

Born: Paddington, 18 July 1968
Celtic career: 1997 to 2003
Appearances and goals:

League		FA Cup		Lg Cup		Europe	
A	G	A	G	A	G	A	G
109/1	0	12	0	14/1	0	21	0

Total appearances: 156/2

Total goals: 0

League Championships: 1997-98; 2000-01
League Cup: 1997-98; 1999-2000; 2000-01
Honours: 2 Scotland caps

The son of former Wales manager Bobby Gould, he was playing for Western League club Clevedon Town before he was signed by Halifax Town in 1990. Later released by the Shaymen, he was signed by his father for West Bromwich Albion, but was not called upon for first-team action.

After being dismissed by Albion, Bobby Gould took charge at Coventry City, and his son was one of his first signings as cover for Steve Ogrizovic. After making his debut in a 5-1 defeat of mighty Liverpool, it all went wrong for him in a game against Wolves at Molineux. Coming off the bench after Ogrizovic had been sent off, he conceded two goals in his first two minutes on the pitch!

Shortly afterwards, he joined Bradford City, but in a game at Molineux—not his happiest ground—he received a face wound requiring 18 stitches! Two sendings-off later during that 1996-97 season restricted his number of appearances for the Bantams.

In the summer of 1997, Gould joined Celtic, and, after missing the opening game of the season, made his debut in a 2-1 home defeat at the hands of Dunfermline Athletic. He went on to play in the remaining 35 games, his 17 clean sheets helping Celtic win the League Championship, two points clear of runners-up Rangers. He was also between the posts that season when Celtic won the League Cup, beating Dundee United 3-0. The club looked like winning the treble, but lost 2-1 to Rangers in the semi-finals of the Scottish Cup.

He won another League Cup winners' medal in 1999-2000 as Celtic beat Aberdeen 2-0, and then in 2000-01 repeated his achievement of three seasons earlier by collecting another League Championship and League Cup winners' medal with another clean sheet in a 3-0 defeat of Kilmarnock. His form was such that season that he won his first full cap for Scotland in the European Championship qualifier against Lithuania which the Scots won 3-0.

After losing out to Rob Douglas, he followed Scotland's national team manager Craig Brown to Preston North End. His displays made him one of the best keepers outside of the Premiership, and though he experienced a number of injuries, he was recalled to the Scotland squad for the Euro 2004 play-offs on the back of some remarkable goalkeeping performances.

Yet at the start of the 2004-05 season following a loan spell at Hereford, his contract was cancelled. Soon afterwards he signed for Bristol City, but did not add to his total of first-team appearances prior to retiring.

PETER GRANT

Born: Bellshill, 30 August 1965
Celtic career: 1982 to 1997
Appearances and goals:

League		FA Cup		Lg Cup		Europe	
A	G	A	G	A	G	A	G
338/26	15	34/4	1	40/3	3	33/1	0

Total appearances: 445/34
Total goals: 19
League Championships: 1985-86; 1987-88
Scottish Cup: 1988-89; 1994-95
Honours: 2 Scotland caps

A whole-hearted midfielder, Peter Grant played every match as if it was his last after being elevated from the Parkhead Boys' Club by manager Billy McNeill following a five-year apprenticeship.

While not exactly shunning the limelight, Grant was more than willing to allow celebrated 'stars' like John Collins and Paul McStay to take the plaudits, while going about the business of containing the opposition with a succession of bone-shaking tackles and precise distribution.

Although sometimes unjustly labelled a workhorse in his early days with the club, Grant's contribution to the team was never questioned. He was even willing to sign 14 month-to-month contracts to stay at Parkhead before being offered a new three-year deal in 1993.

One of his proudest moments came after he suffered an injury which kept him out of the 1988 Scottish Cup Final success over Dundee United. The

Peter Grant during the 1995-1996 season (www.snspix.com)

Hoops had just clinched the League title, but Grant, who had broken his foot at St Mirren a few weeks before, was not playing in the final. A packed house chanted his name until he came out on crutches and joined the team! He was back at Hampden the following year to collect his first winner's medal in a 1-0 victory over Rangers, a badge he was to add to six years later when Celtic beat Airdrie by a similar score—a game in which he thoroughly deserved his Man of the Match award.

On recovering from his broken foot, Grant's form led to him winning full international honours for Scotland, first as a substitute against England in May 1989 and then from the start against Chile three days later.

Again he was hampered by injuries—torn knee ligaments in the game against Aberdeen in January 1994—a game that was eventually abandoned due to fog. This restricted his first team opportunities, but when former team-mate Tommy Burns returned to Parkhead as manager in 1995, he moved quickly to ensure that Grant was not lost to Celtic.

Early in 1997, Peter Grant was rewarded with a testimonial against German giants Bayern Munich, and, despite a bitterly cold night in Glasgow where the temperatures barely got above freezing, almost 40,000 fans filled Parkhead to show their appreciation for his dedicated service to the club for which they shared his love.

A £200,000 transfer took him to Norwich City in the summer of 1997, and during his time at Carrow Road he impressed everyone with his thoroughly professional approach. Allowed to join Reading in 1999, he spent less than a year at the Madejski Stadium before moving to Bournemouth as the Cherries' player-coach. He later retired as a player to become the club's head coach, prior to holding a similar position with West Ham United.

Grant is now manager of Championship side Norwich City, where in his first season in charge, he returned to Parkhead to take Celtic's goalkeeper David Marshall on loan until the end of the 2006-07 season, the move later becoming permanent.

FRANK HAFFEY

Born: Glasgow, 28 November 1938
Celtic career: 1958 to 1964
Appearances and goals:

League		FA Cup		Lg Cup		Europe	
A	G	A	G	A	G	A	G
139	0	34	0	24	0	3	0

Total appearances: 200
Total goals: 0
Honours: 2 Scotland caps

Frank Haffey was a talented goalkeeper, although he was, on occasion, prone to eccentric behaviour! He will forever be saddled with the fact of being Scotland's keeper in the 1961 Wembley debacle, when England crushed the Scots 9-3.

Having begun his career with Greenock Juveniles, he signed for Campsie Black Watch at the start of the 1957-58 season. Celtic's scout Willie Cowan gave him a trial against Rangers' reserve side at Ibrox on New Year's Day 1958, and the club's second team coach at the time, Jock Stein, decided he would like to offer him terms. The following day he met Celtic boss Jimmy McGrory and, after putting pen to paper, was loaned out to Maryhill Harps.

After a number of sound displays for the Hoops, Haffey made his full international debut against England at Hampden Park in April 1960. The game which ended all-square at 1-1 was littered with both free-kicks and throw-ins. England had two penalties, and Bobby Charlton scored one and missed the other. In fact, the Manchester United star missed it twice, Haffey moving before the ball was kicked to save his first effort. The major controversy of the game came when Joe Baker barged Haffey into the net—the referee disallowing the 'goal'.

After the 1961 international, the affable keeper seemed to be in a state of shock. The scoreline gave rise to the joke at the goalkeeper's expense. 'What's the time?' asked one fan. 'Nine past Haffey,' smirked another!

Also in 1961, he was a member of the Celtic side that lost 2-0 to Dunfermline Athletic in the Scottish Cup Final, after the first game had been goalless, and though he reached another Scottish Cup Final with Celtic two years later, he again had to be satisfied with a runners-up medal as Rangers triumphed 3-0 in the replay after a 1-1 draw.

Amongst the keeper's other feats were an own goal when he attempted to steer a free-kick to Dunky MacKay, slicing the ball into his own net, and then, with Celtic beating Airdrie 9-0, hitting a last minute penalty to Roddie McKenzie's left, only to see the Airdrie keeper bring off a marvellous save! Haffey was also one of the first players to record a song.

A broken ankle whilst playing for the Hoops against Partick Thistle at Firhill effectively ended his career at Parkhead, and in October 1964 he turned down the chance to join Third Lanark and moved to Swindon Town for a fee of £8,000. After only a handful of games for the Wiltshire club, he subsequently emigrated to Australia where he starred for a number of clubs, including St George Budapest, Hakoah and Sutherland.

On hanging up his boots, he commenced a new career as a cabaret performer and took a keen interest in Australian Rules Football.

JOHN HARTSON

Born: Swansea, 5 April 1975
Celtic career: 2001 to 2006
Appearances and goals:

League		FA Cup		Lg Cup		Europe	
A	**G**	**A**	**G**	**A**	**G**	**A**	**G**
126/21	87	11/1	8	9/1	7	23/6	6

Total appearances: 169/29
Total goals: 108
League Championships: 2001-02; 2003-04; 2005-06
Scottish Cup: 2004-05
Honours: 50 Wales caps

Welsh international striker John Hartson will always be remembered for his 'hard man' attitude as well as his brilliant goalscoring.

He began his career with Luton Town before joining Arsenal for £2.5 million in January 1995—one of manager George Graham's last signings before his sacking the following month. He was a regular in his first season at Highbury, the highlight of which was scoring Arsenal's equaliser in the 1995 European Cup Winners' Cup Final against Real Zaragoza. However, a last-minute goal from 40 yards by Nayim meant Arsenal lost the game 2-1.

With the signing of Dennis Bergkamp, who was preferred up front to partner Ian Wright, Hartson featured less under Graham's successors Bruce Rioch and Arsene Wenger. With the Frenchman making it clear that Hartson was surplus to requirements, he was sold to West Ham United for £3.2 million.

There was a training ground incident when Hartson was playing for the Hammers in 1998, where he kicked Eyal Berkovic in the head while in front of television cameras. No charges were brought, and the Welshman has admitted in his autobiography that this was an error of judgement.

He later played for Wimbledon and Coventry City before a £6 million transfer took him to Celtic, where he thrived in the Scottish Premier League. In 2001-02, his first season with the Hoops, he helped the club win the League Championship, scoring 19 goals including a hat-trick in a 5-1 defeat of Dundee United. The following season he scored four of Celtic's goals in a 7-0 rout of Aberdeen and another treble as Hearts were beaten 4-2, but a persistent back injury limited his appearances towards the end of the campaign and he not only missed the UEFA Cup Final against Porto, but much of the 2003-04 season as well.

He was given a few red cards in his time, one being a notable dismissal towards the end of an Old Firm derby, when he was sent off for violent conduct along with Celtic team-mate Johan Mjallby and Rangers star Fernando Ricksen.

The 2004-05 season proved to be his best season for the club, helping the Hoops to another League title and top-scoring with 30 goals in all competitions, including a hat-trick in a 4-0 win over Livingston. In April 2005 he shared the Scottish PFA Players' Player of the Year award with Rangers' Fernando Ricksen, and the following month he was voted the Scottish Football Writers' Association Player of the Year.

On 5 April 2006, Hartson scored the winning goal against Hearts on his 31st birthday to clinch yet another title for Celtic, but in the close season, he signed a two-year contract with Championship side West Bromwich Albion, hitting a double on his debut following the £500,000 move. Injuries hampered his progress at the Hawthorns, and there are reports that he will leave the club to finish his playing days with his home-town club, Swansea.

MIKE HAUGHNEY

Born: Paisley, 10 December 1926
Died: Peoria, Illinois, United States, 23 February 2002
Celtic career: 1949 to 1957
Appearances and goals:

League		FA Cup		Lg Cup		Europe	
A	G	A	G	A	G	A	G
159	32	29	5	45	7	-	-

Total appearances: 233
Total goals: 44
League Championships: 1953-54
Scottish Cup: 1953-54
League Cup: 1956-57
Honours: 1 Scotland cap

Football flowed through the veins of Mike Haughney, who played both as a forward and at right-back for the Hoops. His uncle, Andrew Haughney, played, albeit briefly, for Aberdeen, while his great-uncle, Peter Dowds, was one of the first Celtic players.

Mike Haughney grew up in the mining village of Dalkeith, playing his early football with St David's and Newtongrange Star. The Second World War intervened, and in his late teens and early twenties he rose to the rank of captain in the Commando unit of the Seaforth Highlanders.

In 1949 he was signed by Celtic, training with the Parkhead club part-time while also studying for a Bachelor of Commerce degree at the University of Edinburgh. On his Celtic debut in a League Cup tie against Rangers, the scores were level at 2-2 when he netted the winning goal, firing home past a stunned Bobby Brown. He ended his first season as joint-top scorer with John McPhail with 12 goals. When he did eventually lose his place, his first game for the reserves against Raith Rovers saw him fire in a hat-trick in the opening four minutes of the game!

But his truer position was to be as a defender, not a forward, and after a period of injury, he was reinstated into the Celtic side at right-back, playing his first game in this position in a 3-2 defeat of Rangers in the 1950 Danny Kaye Charity Cup Final. He was also at right-back in the Celtic sides that won the St Mungo Cup in 1951 and the Coronation Cup two years later. He also excelled as a redoubtable penalty-taker, scoring 23 out of 25 of Celtic's penalties between 1953 and 1957.

In 1954 he was awarded full international honours when he played in the 4-2 defeat by England at Hampden Park, a match in which West Brom's Ronnie Allen and Johnny Nicholls got amongst the goals. This was the same year that Celtic won the League and Cup double for the first time in 40 years.

He is also remembered, after later reverting to the forward line, for scoring the only, somewhat controversial, goal against Hearts in the whole of their campaign for the Scottish Cup in 1955-56, when in the final the Edinburgh side beat Celtic 3-1.

A year later, Mike Haughney quit football and Scotland. He emigrated to America and took up employment with a bakery firm, and with his blend of intelligence and good humour, worked his way up to a top executive position. He was active in his local church and well known in the community where he lived at Palos Heights, not far from Chicago.

DAVID HAY

Born: Paisley, 29 January 1948
Celtic career: 1966 to 1974
Appearances and goals:

League		FA Cup		Lg Cup		Europe	
A	G	A	G	A	G	A	G
126/3	6	29	1	45	5	25	0

Total appearances: 225/3
Total goals: 12
League Championships: 1969-70; 1970-71; 1971-72; 1972-73; 1973-74
Scottish Cup: 1970-71; 1973-74
League Cup: 1969-70
Honours: 27 Scotland caps

David Hay is well worth his place among the Celtic greats who have graced the green and white hoops over the years. He signed for Celtic in 1966 and was one of the so-called 'Quality Street Kids'—the name given to a Celtic reserve side that included the likes of George Connelly, Kenny Dalglish, Danny McGrain and Lou Macari—who would eventually fill the places left by the ageing Lisbon Lions.

The versatile Hay broke into the first team playing right-back, and made

David Hay in 1970 (www.snspix.com)

an instant impression with his speedy overlaps and eagerness to get involved in the action. Hay was then moved up to midfield by manager Jock Stein and made his mark there too: indeed, he was soon capped in the position by Scotland boss Tommy Docherty, who gave him the label of 'the Quiet Assassin'!

Hay was a member of the Celtic side that won five successive League Championships from 1969-70, a season in which he won his first domestic cup medal as the Hoops beat St Johnstone 1-0 to lift the League Cup. Though he appeared in the next four finals, he was never on the winning side. He did win two Scottish FA Cup winners' medals in 1971 and 1974 as Rangers and Dundee United, respectively, were beaten.

Hay suffered a bad injury in a Scottish Cup replay against Hearts at Tynecastle in March 1973, and was out of the game for a lengthy period. On his return to action, he pleaded for a better deal for injured players, and when this fell on deaf ears, he put in his first transfer request. He even refused to train, but eventually the differences were patched up and he saw out the season prior to the 1974 World Cup Finals with a series of unforgettable performances. In July 1974, immediately after the World Cup Finals, in which he was Scotland's most outstanding player, Hay joined Chelsea for a fee of £225,000, making him London's most expensive footballer. It took him some time to settle into his new surroundings, and after undergoing surgery for the removal of a cataract, he found he was still not sure of a place in the Chelsea starting line-up. Eventually paired with Steve Wicks at the heart of the Chelsea defence, he played his part in helping the Stamford Bridge club win promotion to the First Division in 1976-77.

Further problems with his eye threatened to curtail his career, but after no fewer than three operations to repair a detached retina, the courageous player made a comeback. However, he then suffered a knee injury that forced his premature retirement a year later.

Hay then moved into management as boss of Motherwell, before, in the summer of 1983, becoming Celtic supremo in succession to Billy McNeill. He stayed at Parkhead for four seasons, which yielded the Scottish Cup in 1985 and a dramatic last day League Championship triumph in 1986, when a 5-0 victory against St Mirren handed his team the title after Hearts had lost at Dundee.

In 1987 Hay made way for McNeill to return to Parkhead, and after a season as boss of St Mirren, took up a coaching appointment in America as youth director of Tampa Bay Rowdies. He later became assistant-manager of Swindon Town, but resigned after a year before being given the position of chief scout at Celtic by Tommy Burns. Unfortunately, like many others, he fell foul of Fergus McCann.

Hay later managed Livingston to League Cup glory in 2004, but left soon after to take over the reins of Dunfermline Athletic. He resigned his post shortly before the end of the 2004-05 season.

HARRY HOOD

Born: Glasgow, 3 October 1944
Celtic career: 1969 to 1976
Appearances and goals:

League		FA Cup		Lg Cup		Europe	
A	**G**	**A**	**G**	**A**	**G**	**A**	**G**
161/29	74	25/4	13	53/12	24	24/6	12

Total appearances: 263/51
Total goals: 123
League Championships: 1969-70; 1970-71; 1971-72; 1972-73; 1973-74
Scottish Cup: 1970-71; 1973-74; 1974-75
League Cup: 1969-70; 1974-75

Harry Hood playing in the 1971 League Cup Final between Celtic and Partick Thistle—which Celtic unexpectedly lost (www.snspix.com)

Harry Hood, whose presence on the pitch at Parkhead was invariably greeted by the 'Hare Krishna' chant, was always destined to turn out in the green and white of Celtic, but the reason he had to wait until he was approaching his 25th birthday before pulling on the hoops remains a mystery. Glasgow-born Hood was frequently linked with a move to Parkhead before he arrived in a £40,000 deal from Clyde in March 1969, after a short spell playing alongside Jim Baxter at Sunderland.

Harry Hood, a lifelong Celtic fan, was a Jock Stein-type player—a beautifully balanced artist blessed with superb ball control. Add to this an unerring knack of finding the net against Rangers, and it is not hard to see why he became an instant hit with the Celtic fans.

He tasted defeat against the Light Blues in one of his very first games for the club, although he did manage the counter in a 2-1 reverse. But the following month, October 1969, he grabbed the only goal of a stormy match and as far as the fans were concerned, this was the moment he became one of them.

No player at the time, not even Jinky Johnstone or Billy McNeill, had the ability to goad the Jungle into full voice quite like Harry Hood. He scored some stunning goals for the Hoops—a bullet header in the second round of the 1969-70 European Cup campaign against Benfica enhanced his love affair with the supporters.

He scored some vital goals too during the 1970-71 season—an important early strike against Aberdeen at Pittodrie that gave Celtic a 1-1 draw there and did much to ensure the League Championship came to Parkhead, and then, later in the season, an ice-cool conversion of a penalty-kick against Rangers in the replayed Scottish Cup Final. That season saw him finish as Scotland's leading marksman with 22 league goals.

Hood had Rangers on the run again when grabbing all three goals in a 3-1 League Cup semi-final victory in December 1973. He won five League Championship medals, three Scottish Cup and two League Cup winners' medals but, incredibly, he was never capped by Scotland at full international level. He did play four times in the unofficial world tour of 1967 and scored against England in his only Under-23 game at Hampden.

Hood was freed in April 1976 and joined NASL side San Antonio Thunder the following month. After an unproductive spell with Motherwell, he ended his playing career with Queen of the South. In the early 1980s, Hood had brief unsuccessful spells in management with Albion Rovers and Queen of the South. He later quit and now runs the Angels Hotel in Uddingston.

PIERRE VAN HOOIJDONK

Born: Steenbergen, Holland, 29 November 1969
Celtic career: 1994 to 1997
Appearances and goals:

League		FA Cup		Lg Cup		Europe	
A	G	A	G	A	G	A	G
66/3	44	11	9	6	3	6/2	0

Total appearances: 89/5
Total goals: 62
Scottish Cup: 1994-95
Honours: 46 Holland caps

Pierre Van Hooijdonk wrote himself into the Celtic history books before a bitter contract wrangle ended his all-too-brief stay at Parkhead. The big Dutch striker became an instant hit with the Hoops fans, scoring a stunning debut goal against Hearts following his £1.2 million move from NAC Breda in January 1995. A lethal dead-ball expert and an aerial threat to the best of defences, Van Hooijdonk grabbed a further seven goals, including the only strike in the Scottish Cup Final victory over Airdrie, before the season was over.

Van Hooijdonk started his career at Roosendaal before moving to Breda, where his goals helped them lift the coveted Dutch Team of the Season award in 1993-94. He had scored 81 goals in 115 games for Breda before his arrival at Parkhead.

In 1994-95, his only full season for the club, Van Hooijdonk took up where he left off the previous campaign, becoming the first Celt in almost a decade to find the net over 30 times. His 32-goal haul helped him earn a call-up for the Dutch side, a chance he grabbed with both hands by scoring twice in a 3-1 World Cup qualifying victory over Wales at Ninian Park.

Portuguese striker Jorge Cadete arrived from Sporting Lisbon to form the partnership manager Tommy Burns hoped would deliver the League Championship to Parkhead after a nine-year absence. But the pairing barely had a chance to gel before Van Hooijdonk, upset at his wage level compared to other top players at the club, became involved in a war of words with chairman Fergus McCann. Van Hooijdonk stated that the reputed £7,000 a week he was being offered might be 'good enough for the homeless' to live on, 'but not for an international striker'.

This ended with him moving to the English Premiership side Nottingham Forest, who, languishing at the foot of the table, paid £3.5 million for his services. Though he was unable to save them from relegation, he immediately pledged his future to helping the club regain their top flight status.

The following season was an unqualified success both for Van Hooijdonk and Forest. The club won the title and promotion in a competitive league, and the Dutchman scored 34 goals after building up a good rapport with strike partner Kevin Campbell. After playing for Holland in the 1998 World Cup, he found that the promised strengthening of Forest's squad had not transpired, and so he asked for a transfer. The club's new owners would not let him leave, with the result that van Hooijdonk announced he would be going on strike, though he kept fit by training with his former club NAC Breda.

He received criticism both from fans and from his team-mates for his actions, and the stand-off continued until early November 1998, when he had no choice but to return. At the end of that 1998-99 season, he returned to Holland with Vitesse Arnhem, before spending a season with Benfica. After the 2000-01 campaign he signed for his fourth Dutch club, Feyenoord, whom he helped win the UEFA Cup. Never one to settle down, Van

Hooijdonk joined Fenerbahce before returning to NAC Breda and finally ending his career with another former club, Feyenoord.

Van Hooijdonk repeatedly knocked back offer upon offer to join Celtic's arch-rivals Rangers, due to a healthy respect for his former club.

JOHN HUGHES

Born: Coatbridge, 3 April 1943
Celtic career: 1959 to 1971
Appearances and goals:

League		FA Cup		Lg Cup		Europe	
A	G	A	G	A	G	A	G
252/3	116	50/1	25	68/1	38	38/2	10

Total appearances: 408/7
Total goals: 189
League Championships: 1965-66; 1966-67; 1967-68; 1968-69; 1969-70; 1970-71
Scottish Cup: 1964-65
League Cup: 1965-66; 1966-67; 1967-68; 1969-70
Honours: 8 Scotland caps

John 'Yogi' Hughes had the ability both to infuriate and delight Celtic fans on a minute-to-minute basis. The burly striker, nicknamed after the lovable cartoon character, was described as powerful and frightening one week, slow and cumbersome the next, and came in for more than his fair share of barracking from impatient terrace-goers. However, John Hughes' commitment and popularity as a Hoop can never be called into question.

He joined Celtic as a 17-year-old from Shotts Bon Accord in 1960, and, within two weeks of scoring against Third Lanark in the League Cup, he had gained the respect of the hard-to-please Parkhead terrace purists. The hitman turned on the style again seven days later to score in a classic 3-2 win over Rangers at Ibrox.

Too much was expected of him, and nobody could live up to those expectations. However, by most standards his career has to be considered outstanding. Having had a great game for the Scottish League against the Football League at Hampden Park on St Patrick's Day 1965, when he scored two and gave Jack Charlton a torrid time, he was selected for his first full international against Spain the following May. It was a bruising encounter, but Hughes, playing at outside-left, gave as good as he got and went on to win eight caps for his country.

For Celtic, Hughes scored some memorable goals—one goal, a long mazy run beating four defenders and ending up with a most powerful shot, against Morton at Greenock in the 1964 Scottish Cup, was described by his manager Jimmy McGrory as the best individual goal he had ever witnessed; a glancing header against Leeds United at Hampden helped Celtic through

John 'Yogi' Hughes in action during the 1967-68 season. Note the proximity of the wall to the touchline! (www.snspix.com)

to the European Cup Final in 1970, while two penalty-kicks converted against Rangers in the 1965 League Cup Final capped off a marvellous day for Hughes.

On another memorable afternoon in 1965, Celtic absolutely demolished Aberdeen 8-0 on an icy pitch, with 'Yogi', wearing white sandshoes, scoring an astonishing five of his side's goals!

Although Hughes was dropped from the side which won the European Cup in 1967, he was awarded a winners' medal in recognition of the part he played in the team and for having played in the requisite number of matches to qualify for a medal, along with Joe McBride and Charlie Gallacher.

Along with Willie Wallace, he moved to Crystal Palace in 1971 for a fee of £30,000, and one of his goals in the game against Sheffield United in December 1971 was featured over and over again as one of the goals of the season. He later joined his brother Billy at Sunderland, but he had made just one appearance for the Wearsiders when injury forced his retirement.

After coaching Baillieston FC he became manager of Stranraer, later becoming the Scottish Junior FA's first international team manager. 'Yogi' now runs a public bar only a free-kick from Parkhead!

MO JOHNSTON

Born: Glasgow, 13 April 1963
Celtic career: 1984 to 1987
Appearances and goals:

League		FA Cup		Lg Cup		Europe	
A	**G**	**A**	**G**	**A**	**G**	**A**	**G**
97/2	52	14	6	8	9	6	4

Total appearances: 125/2
Total goals: 71
League Championships: 1985-86
Scottish Cup: 1984-85
Honours: 38 Scotland caps

Mo Johnston could not have caused a bigger furore than he did when becoming the first well-known Roman Catholic to sign for Rangers in the summer of 1989. 'Celtic are the only team I ever wanted to play for,' he had said shortly before, after being paraded in the club's shirt by manager Billy McNeill, who had brought him 'home' from a three-year exile in France!

An apprentice cutter before making the grade with Partick Thistle in 1981, he departed for Watford two years later for a fee of £200,000. But after one free-scoring year at Vicarage Road where he teamed up alongside John Barnes—netting a hat-trick against Wolves and scoring 20 goals in 29 games—he became the most expensive player in the Scottish Premier League when Celtic brought him back to Scotland for £400,000 in October 1984.

Mojo made his debut against Hibernian before opening his account the following week in a 3-1 win against Dundee United at Tannadice. It wasn't long before he was showing all the attributes of a truly world-class striker: pace, vision and strength. He was good in the air and particularly sharp in and around the six-yard box. Johnston ended his first season at Parkhead with a Scottish Cup winners' medal after Celtic had beaten Dundee United 2-1.

The following season, 1985-86, saw Celtic win the League Championship, pipping Hearts on the last day of the campaign. The margin was on goal-difference, as the Hoops beat St Mirren 5-0 at Love Street and Hearts fell to two late goals from Dundee at Dens Park. In October 1986, Johnson was sent off in the Skol Cup Final against Rangers with just two minutes left. Celtic lost 2-1 after extra-time, and Johnson infuriated Rangers' fans by blessing himself as he left the field!

Johnston moved to Nantes in the summer of 1987, and spent a couple of seasons there before deciding on a return to Parkhead. However, within days, 'Mojo' had defected to the other side of the city, much to the disgust of the Celtic faithful, half the Rangers fans and, if former Light Blues skipper Terry Butcher is to be believed, a good few of the staff at Ibrox as well. When Johnston was introduced on Rangers' tour of Italy, all the English players made him feel at home. But he wasn't accepted by the Scottish lads, and even the club's kit man refused to lay out his kit for training!

After his return to Glasgow, Mo Johnston became something of a journeyman, with spells at Everton, Hearts and Falkirk, before opting for a switch to the United States and Major League Soccer in 1996.

Signing for Kansas City Wiz, he was part of the team that won the MLS Cup in 2000. A year later he retired, and from 2003 to 2005 was assistant coach for the Metro Stars. After a spell as interim head coach he was promoted to the full-time position with re-branded Red Bull New York. After a disappointing start to the following season he was fired, but has since been appointed as head coach of Toronto FC.

JIMMY JOHNSTONE

Born: Glasgow, 30 September 1944
Died: 13 March 2006
Celtic career: 1961 to 1975
Appearances and goals:

League		FA Cup		Lg Cup		Europe	
A	G	A	G	A	G	A	G
298/10	82	47/1	11	87/5	21	63/1	16

Total appearances: 495/17
Total goals: 130
League Championships: 1965-66; 1966-67; 1967-68; 1968-69; 1969-70; 1970-71; 1971-72; 1972-73; 1973-74
Scottish Cup: 1966-67; 1970-71; 1971-72; 1973-74
League Cup: 1965-66; 1966-67; 1968-69; 1969-70; 1974-75
European Cup: 1966-67
Honours: 23 Scotland caps

Jimmy Johnstone is without doubt the greatest winger ever produced in Scotland. Though many will argue a case for the likes of Alan Morton and Willie Henderson, when on form Jimmy Johnstone had no equals. 'Jinky' was capable of leaving entire opposing defences in shreds with his close ball

Jimmy Johnstone on the attack during the 1966-67 season (www.snspix.com)

control and trademark mazy runs. And, unlike many contemporaries, a fine cross or pinpoint cut-back was usually the culmination of his efforts.

Johnstone had been a ball-boy at Parkhead at the age of 13, before joining the full-time staff in November 1961 and becoming an instant favourite with the Celtic fans.

He starred for Celtic on countless occasions—the League decider against Rangers when he scored both goals in the Ibrox mudbath of May 1967, the torment of Leeds United's Terry Cooper in the semi-final of the 1970 European Cup, and, in the dark blue of Scotland, the 2-0 victory over England at Hampden three months before the 1974 World Cup Finals.

But in the eyes of many Celtic fans, the night Jinky really turned it on was against Red Star Belgrade in November 1968. With the team drawing 1-1 at half-time, Celtic boss Jock Stein told Johnstone, who hated flying, that he would not have to travel to Belgrade for the second leg if the team gained a big enough lead. Johnstone went on to run riot in the second half, scoring twice and setting up another two goals in an unforgettable 5-1 victory.

Johnstone had a capacity for getting into scrapes both on and off the pitch. In his early days at Parkhead, he was suspended by Jock Stein for lunging at an opponent; in 1974, as Scotland's preparations for the World Cup were undermined by constant stories of indiscipline, Johnstone was found drifting in a rowing boat without a paddle in the small hours of the morning! The coastguard had to be called to rescue him. On his return to the hotel, Johnstone remarked, 'Don't know what all the fuss is about—I thought I'd go fishing!'

Yet no-one doubted his ability. His contribution to Celtic's victory in the 1967 European Cup Final was immense. Helenio Herrera, Inter Milan's astute manager, put his top defender Burgnich on Jinky. The seasoned international endured a 90-minute nightmare as the Scot twisted, turned and tantalised throughout the game. Defenders watched and took note.

Subsequently, Johnstone was to be tested by the hard men of two continents. A year later in the World Club Championship against the disgraceful Argentinean team Racing Club, Johnstone retaliated to the most horrendous of tackles and was sent off—the first of three Celtic players to go in a farcical third match. In the notorious 1974 European Cup semi-final against Atletico Madrid, Johnstone was continually tripped and hacked, and, as he left the field, he was kicked in the stomach. In the second leg in Madrid, he was given two black eyes by Spanish elbows, yet still kept his head when retaliation would have been only too human.

He left Parkhead in 1975 for the San Jose Earthquakes, before later starring briefly for Sheffield United, Dundee, Shelbourne and Elgin City before hanging up his boots.

His dry wit was in evidence when the Lisbon Lions were paraded at Parkhead on the occasion of the 25th anniversary of their triumph in the European Cup. Paul McStay, the then Celtic skipper and an excellent player in a poor Hoops side, asked Jinky who he thought would win if the 1967 team was to play the Celtic team of 1992. Johnstone paused to consider for a moment, then he replied he thought it would be a draw. McStay suggested that perhaps the veteran was being kind to the current team. Johnstone explained, 'Well, you've got to remember that we're all in our fifties now!'

In November 2001, Jinky was diagnosed with motor neurone disease, and in March 2006 he sadly lost his battle. Thousands of Celtic fans and fans of other clubs, including arch-rivals Rangers, paid tribute to his memory outside Parkhead on St Patrick's Day, the day of his funeral service. Tributes were paid to Johnstone before the League Cup Final—there was a minute of applause before the game and the entire Celtic squad wore the number 7 on both the front and back of their shorts in his honour. Also, when the match ended, as part of the celebrations for winning the match, they all put on tops displaying JINKY and the number 7.

JIM KENNEDY

Born: Johnstone, 31 January 1934
Celtic career: 1955 to 1965
Appearances and goals:

League		FA Cup		Lg Cup		Europe	
A	G	A	G	A	G	A	G
170	0	29	0	31	2	11	0

Total appearances: 241
Total goals: 2
Honours: 6 Scotland caps

A huge supporter of the Hoops as a boy, Jim Kennedy left school and joined a Celtic Supporters Club. The youngster had no desire to play football whatsoever, and in fact made little or no attempt even to take the game seriously until he undertook his National Service in Belgium!

But even then, on his return to these shores he only joined his local club Johnstone Glencairn, and that was some six months after leaving the armed forces. He then had a brief spell with Duntocher Hibernian before joining his beloved Hoops. Kennedy made his debut at left-back against Partick Thistle, coming up against the Jags' flying international winger Johnny McKenzie. Though Thistle won 2-0, Kennedy had an outstanding debut, and it wasn't long before he established himself as first team regular at Parkhead.

Kennedy produced some remarkable displays in the Celtic defence, perhaps none more than the Charity Cup game against Clyde in May 1956, and then four years later in the Old Firm game against Rangers. In fact, Kennedy's display that day led to talk of him winning full international honours. Unfortunately it wasn't to be, and worse was to come for the young defender. He had just given up his job in an Elderslie carpet factory to go full-time when he suffered appendicitis, and was forced miss the Cup Final replay against Dunfermline Athletic.

At the beginning of the 1963-64 season, Kennedy was dropped in favour of Tommy Gemmell, but it wasn't too long before he received a new lease of life. In October of that season, Kennedy was moved to left-half where he gave a series of commanding performances. His displays led to him finally winning full international honours, but when the Celtic left-half did turn out for the national side against Wales, it was at left-back!

Having helped Scotland beat Wales 2-1, he kept his place in the side for the visit of England to Hampden Park, and played his part in a 1-0 win. Kennedy, who went on to win six full caps, held his place in the Celtic side until the appointment of the legendary Jock Stein as the club's new manager, when John Clark became the preferred option.

Though he didn't manage to win any domestic honours, Jim Kennedy made 241 first team appearances for the Hoops, as well as having a spell on loan with Rangers. Eventually he left Parkhead in November 1965 to join Morton. In his first full season at Cappielow Park, Kennedy, who had been appointed the club's captain, led his team to promotion.

In the summer of 1968, Jim Kennedy was appointed liaison officer between Celtic and the Supporters Clubs, but re-signed as a reserve for a one-off game against his former club Morton the following evening!

PAUL LAMBERT

Born: Glasgow, 7 August 1969
Celtic career: 1997 to 2005
Appearances and goals:

League		FA Cup		Lg Cup		Europe	
A	G	A	G	A	G	A	G
180/13	14	19/4	1	10/1	2	44/3	2

Total appearances: 253/21
Total goals: 19
League Championships: 1997-98; 2000-01; 2001-02; 2003-04
Scottish Cup: 2000-01
League Cup: 1997-98; 1999-2000; 2000-01
Honours: 40 Scotland caps

Affectionately nicknamed 'The Kaiser' as a result of his incredibly successful time in Germany with Borussia Dortmund, Paul Lambert started out with junior side Linwood Rangers in 1984, before entering the professional game with St Mirren.

He had represented Scotland at Under-21 level while at Love Street, and spent eight years with the Paisley club before transferring to Motherwell. It was the beginning of a few seasons in which the Steelmen had a wonderful midfield. Both elegant and economical, Lambert won the first of his 40 full caps for Scotland against Japan, but left Fir Park under the Bosman Ruling in the summer of 1996. The move was hard for Motherwell to bear, because Lambert at that time was probably worth in excess of £1 million.

Transferring to the German Bundesliga side Borussia Dortmund, Lambert was well liked by the fans in Germany and contributed to the team's success in winning the 1997 UEFA Champions League in the final against Juventus in Munich. He quelled the threat of Zinedine Zidane, and Dortmund won 3-1, making Lambert the first British player to get a Champions League winners' medal.

In November 1997, after just over a year playing in the Bundesliga, he was signed by Celtic for a fee in the region of £2 million. In his first season at Parkhead, he helped the Hoops win the League Championship and the League Cup, when he came off the bench to help Celtic beat Dundee United 3-0. He went on to help Celtic win four Premier Division titles in

Paul Lambert, then Celtic captain, takes the ball away from Derek Townsley of Hibernian during a 2003 SPL game (www.snspix.com)

his time at Parkhead, along with three League Cups and the Scottish Cup in 2001, when Hibernian were also defeated 3-0.

Celtic's captain and a steadying influence both on and off the field, he was voted the Scottish Football Writers' Footballer of the Year in 2002, but after that occasionally found himself left out of the side by Martin O'Neill as the Celtic boss accommodated Chris Sutton in midfield. One of the club's most influential players of recent years, he played a great part in helping the Hoops reach the 2003 UEFA Cup Final in Seville.

Capped 40 times by Scotland, he played in the 1998 World Cup, turning in an especially impressive performance as the Scots lost 2-1 to Brazil at the Stade de France in the tournament's opening match.

After studying for football coaching qualifications in 2005, Lambert landed his first managerial job with Livingston. He studied for his UEFA coaching credentials in Germany, one of very few non-Germans to have been given dispensation to do so. In February 2006, after a poor run of results, Lambert resigned his post with Livingston and was replaced by former Hearts boss, John Robertson.

In the summer of 2006, Lambert was appointed manager of Wycombe Wanderers and led them to the League Cup semi-finals, with a 1-0 away win over Premiership side Charlton Athletic. It was the first time a club from the fourth tier of English football had reached that stage for over 30 years. They also held champions Chelsea to a 1-1 draw at Adams Park.

Paul Lambert's determination and contribution to the Celtic side are undisputed and the Parkhead club's fans will forever be appreciative for the success brought by this talented, down-to-earth, but inspiring, player.

HENRIK LARSSON

Born: Helsingborg, Sweden, 20 September 1971
Celtic career: 1997 to 2004
Appearances and goals:

League		FA Cup		Lg Cup		Europe	
A	G	A	G	A	G	A	G
218/3	174	25	23	11	10	58	35

Total appearances: 312/3
Total goals: 242
League Championships: 1997-98; 2000-01; 2001-02; 2003-04
Scottish Cup: 2000-01; 2003-04
League Cup: 1997-98; 2000-01
Honours: 93 Sweden caps

Henrik Larsson's phenomenal strike-rate for Celtic compares favourably with almost any of the game's greatest goalscorers.

Larsson started his professional career playing for Hopgaborg. He subsequently moved to Helsingborg IF, where he scored 50 goals in 56 appearances. It was this sensational form that attracted Dutch club Feyenoord, who signed him for £295,000 in 1993. This was despite the fact that he was negotiating a contract with Grasshopper-Club Zurich at the time!

Following a complicated contractual dispute with Feyenoord, he was signed by Celtic manager Wim Jansen in the summer of 1997 for a fee of £650,000. His debut against Hibernian at Easter Road was less than spectacular: he inadvertently passed the ball to Hibs player, Chic Charnley, resulting in a 2-1 defeat for the Hoops! He didn't fare much better in his first European game either, scoring an own goal, although Celtic did run out winners 6-3. On the final day of the 1997-98 season, Celtic needed to beat St Johnstone at a packed Parkhead to claim the League title for the first time in a decade. It was Larsson who calmed everyone's nerves after a tense opening, with an exquisite curling shot from the far corner of the penalty area past the St Johnstone keeper's despairing dive.

Henrik Larsson was crowned Scotland's best player in 1999 by both the

Henrik Larsson in full flow during a 2003 SPL match against Livingston
(www.snspix.com)

Scottish PFA and the Scottish Football Writers' Association, winning both of these awards a second time in 2001.

In October 1999, disaster struck as Larsson, playing in a UEFA Cup tie in Lyon against Olympique Lyonnais, suffered a horrific injury, breaking his leg in two places. Though he was out of action for more than a year, the player, who celebrates a goal by amusingly sticking out his tongue, bounced back better than ever.

In 2000-01, he won the 'Golden Boot' award for being Europe's most prolific goalscorer with 35 league goals—including four against Kilmarnock and hat-tricks against Aberdeen and Hearts. His total in all competitions was an amazing 53 as Celtic took the treble. Also that season he netted four goals for Sweden in a 6-0 World Cup qualifying win over Moldova—this total included the unusual feat of a hat-trick of penalties!

Larsson's international record is impressive, with 36 goals in 93 games, many of which he played in midfield or as a winger. He always made his mark on big occasions, and has scored at three World Cup Finals and two European Championships. He chose to retire from international football in 2002, but there was much clamouring for him to return and he eventually came back to the national side at the behest of his son. He retired from international football for a second time in the summer of 2006, but even now there is talk of Swedish boss Lars Lagerback trying to lure him out of international retirement!

In 2003, he scored two superb goals in the UEFA Cup Final, although opponents Porto went on to win 3-2. His goalscoring feats on the continent for Celtic mean he holds the record number of goals scored for a club from the British Isles in European matches. Celtic fans voted him the only foreigner in the greatest-ever Celtic team. In his last appearance for Celtic, he scored twice to help defeat Dunfermline Athletic and win the Scottish Cup. He later made a tearful farewell at his testimonial match against Sevilla.

Larsson's first season with Barcelona was plagued by injury, and he played only a nominal part in Barca's La Liga win. He did, however, score against the Hoops in a Champions League match. In his second season with the club, he scored 10 goals as Barcelona won la Liga for a second consecutive year. Midway through the campaign, he announced that at the end of his contract he would return to Sweden to end his career. In his final game for Barcelona, he won his first UEFA Champions League medal, coming off the bench to have a hand in both of his side's goals in a 2-1 win over Arsenal.

After a short stint with Helsingborg IF, Larsson was signed on loan by Sir Alex Ferguson's Manchester United. Though both club and player would have liked him to stay and see the season out, he had promised his family and his club that he would return to Sweden in March. Henrik Larsson is such an established player, respected and admired, that only days after finishing his loan spell with United, he was called upon to captain a

European XI against Manchester United in the fixture in celebration of the Old Trafford club's 50 years of association with UEFA.

NEIL LENNON

Born: Lurgan, Northern Ireland, 25 June 1971
Celtic career: 2000 to 2007
Appearances and goals:

League		FA Cup		Lg Cup		Europe	
A	G	A	G	A	G	A	G
212/2	3	26	0	10/1	0	52/1	0

Total appearances: 300/4
Total goals: 3
League Championships: 2000-01; 2001-02; 2003-04; 2005-06; 2006-07
Scottish Cup: 2000-01; 2004-05; 2006-07
League Cup: 2005-06
Honours: 40 Northern Ireland caps

When Martin O'Neill paid £6 million to take Neil Lennon north of the Border from his former club Leicester City in 2000, no-one could have predicted the impact the Irishman would have at Parkhead. A terrier-like figure, Lennon has been a constant source of inspiration for his team-mates and supporters over the past seven seasons.

Briefly on the books of Manchester City, the midfielder made his name with Crewe Alexandra, where he became an important member of the Railwaymen's side. Easily recognised by his red hair, he was capped by Northern Ireland at several levels while at Gresty Road, and his consistency also saw him selected by fellow professionals both in 1994 and 1995 to the teams that won the PFA Divisional Awards.

Ambitious for a higher grade of football, he joined First Division Leicester City for a fee of £750,000 in February 1996, and gave an outstanding performance at Wembley as the Foxes reached the Premiership via the play-offs. Lennon was also elected to the PFA award-winning Second Division team before he joined Leicester for a third year running. The following season, his impressive non-stop displays against Middlesbrough in the League Cup Final both at Wembley and in the replay at Hillsbrough were a major factor in City lifting the trophy for the first time since the competition began.

Lennon continued to develop as a key member of the midfield for both club and country, and in 1999-2000 helped Leicester to another League Cup win as they beat Tranmere Rovers in the final, running Matt Elliott close for the Man of the Match award.

In 2000-01, Lennon played amid mounting speculation about an impending transfer to Celtic. He eventually linked up with his former mentor Martin

O'Neill in December, and, in his first season, helped the Hoops to a League and Cup double. A key figure in the Hoops' various silverware acquisitions since, he was made Celtic captain and was a central figure in their journey to the 2003 UEFA Cup Final, where Celtic were eventually beaten 3-2 by Porto.

A regular for Northern Ireland, he was treated disgracefully by some sections of his own supporters during a subsequent World Cup tie in Belfast because of his Catholic background and his new club allegiance, but showed great character to put those incidents behind him as the sporting world rallied in his support. Lennon continued to win silverware with the Parkhead club, but sadly, after making 40 appearances for Northern Ireland, decided to retire somewhat prematurely from international football.

The 2004-05 season saw him continue to be integral to Celtic's success, and he remained a rock in midfield, playing a gruelling 49 games throughout the club's domestic and European campaigns. The following season saw no decline in the captain's influence as he led the Hoops to the SPL title and the League Cup. After intense speculation that he would move back to England, he was convinced by Gordon Strachan to sign a new contract.

Though he was linked with a possible move to Crystal Palace in a player/coach role, Celtic announced he had signed a new one-year contract. One of the club's most committed players, Neil Lennon, who led the Hoops to yet another League and Scottish Cup double in 2006-07, left Parkhead in the summer and joined Nottingham Forest on a one-year deal.

BOBBY LENNOX

Born: Saltcoats, 30 August 1943
Celtic career: 1962 to 1980
Appearances and goals:

League		FA Cup		Lg Cup		Europe	
A	G	A	G	A	G	A	G
297/50	168	47/5	31	107/14	63	54/12	14

Total appearances: 505/81
Total goals: 276
League Championships: 1965-66; 1966-67; 1967-68; 1968-69; 1969-70; 1970-71; 1971-72; 1972-73; 1973-74; 1978-79
Scottish Cup: 1964-65; 1966-67; 1968-69; 1970-71; 1971-72; 1973-74; 1974-75; 1979-80
League Cup: 1965-66; 1966-67; 1967-68; 1968-69
European Cup: 1966-67
Honours: 10 Scotland caps

Bobby Lennox was a striker whose devastating speed and unerring eye for goal terrorised the best defences at home and abroad throughout the 1960s and 1970s.

Born in Saltcoats, Bobby Lennox was the only Lisbon Lion not born

Bobby Lennox (right) and Jimmy Johnstone race forward in a match during the 1965-66 season (www.snspix.com)

within 30 miles of Glasgow. After a spell with Ardeer Recreation, he signed professional forms for Celtic in September 1961 and, in March of the following year, made his debut in a 2-1 home win over Dundee. But he was far from fulfilling his potential at Parkhead before the arrival of Jock Stein, who moved him from an out-and-out left-winger into the middle of the park alongside Steve Chalmers.

The switch worked wonders for 'Lemon' who, thriving on an endless supply of ammunition from Bertie Auld and Bobby Murdoch, went on to set a post-war scoring record for the club of 276 goals in 586 appearances in all competitions.

Lennox, like captain Billy McNeill, had the knack of scoring vital goals, notably his last-minute efforts in the League deciders of 1966 and 1968, but it is a disallowed effort in the semi-final of the European Cup Winners' Cup against Liverpool that still haunts him to this day. 'I could not possibly have been offside. I ran past two of the players,' he pleaded after the 2-0 defeat. 'They had their heads in their hands knowing we were through to the final.'

After being preferred to John Hughes for the 1967 European Cup Final, Lennox had one of his best games for the club in the 2-1 victory over Inter Milan, giving the Italians' defence a torrid time. However, in the World Club Championship play-off in Montevideo in November 1967, he was sent off but later exonerated by the Scottish FA as a case of mistaken identity. In fact, on New Year's Day 1974 in the match against Clyde, he was booked for the first time in 12 years.

Lennox scored in three consecutive Scottish Cup Finals (1969-1971)—a remarkable achievement for a player who was supposedly on his way out of Parkhead at the time of Jock Stein's appointment. He won 10 League Championship medals, eight Scottish Cup medals and four League Cup medals as well as 10 full caps for Scotland. He is one of the small band of Scotsmen to play in two European Cup Finals, and also one of the few to have scored in a Scotland victory over England at Wembley, scoring one of the goals in the famous 3-2 victory in 1967.

Lennox, also known as 'Buzz Bomb', left Celtic in the late seventies and moved to the United States to play for Houston Hurricane. He returned to Parkhead in 1979—it was a good move as the Hoops took the League Championship that year and the Scottish Cup in 1980.

Awarded the MBE in 1981, he was inducted into the Scottish Football Museum Hall of Fame in November 2005, and continues his connection with Celtic as a match day host, and is the Honorary President of the Houston Bobby Lennox Supporters Club!

LOU MACARI

Born: Edinburgh, 4 June 1949
Celtic career: 1966 to 1973
Appearances and goals:

League		FA Cup		Lg Cup		Europe	
A	G	A	G	A	G	A	G
58	27	8	8	24	14	12	8

Total appearances: 102

Total goals: 57
League Championships: 1969-70; 1971-72
Scottish Cup: 1970-71; 1971-72
Honours: 24 Scotland caps

A Quality Street Gang member of considerable talent, Luigi Macari was the son of an Italian chip-shop owner. He broke into the Celtic team before his old pals Danny McGrain and Kenny Dalglish, making his place secure almost immediately when he demonstrated a more than useful knack of putting the ball into the net.

It was Macari's dramatic winner in the 1971 Scottish Cup Final, after coming off the bench for Willie Wallace, which edged out rivals Rangers in a 2-1 win and put him on the Scottish football map. Macari's all-action style, snapping at defenders' heels, was eye-catching and Scotland honours followed quickly.

He would surely have gone on to even greater things with the Hoops but for a falling out with manager Jock Stein over money—this while he was midway through a five-year contract. In the end, he left Parkhead in early 1973 to join Manchester United for a then-Scottish record £200,000 transfer fee—and, coincidentally or otherwise, the club's era of success was about to draw to a close. Macari had won two Championship and Scottish Cup medals and appeared in three successive League Cup Finals.

He was never one to shy away from publicity, and he was eventually banned from the Scotland side after a night out with five other team-mates while on World Cup duty in Copenhagen!

A player of great flair, Macari was part of United's attractive side of the mid-1970s. However, at the end of his first season at Old Trafford, the club were relegated for the first time in 37 years. Macari scored the only goal of the victory over Southampton which secured the club's promotion back to the top flight at the first attempt. Then, after playing in the 1976 FA Cup Final defeat, he had a major hand in victory over Liverpool in the following season's final, when his shot was deflected over the line by Jimmy Greenhoff for the winning goal. Two years later he was back at Wembley when United lost 3-2 to Arsenal, but by the mid-1980s, he had made way for younger men.

He then began a rollercoaster managerial career, which saw him in trouble with the FA while at Swindon Town for his alleged involvement in a betting scandal. After spells with West Ham United, Birmingham City and Stoke, Macari came back to his roots in 1993 when he stepped into Liam Brady's shoes to become Celtic manager. But despite a 2-1 Old Firm win in his first game in charge, things did not go well and he was sacked by Fergus McCann, who claimed he didn't fulfil his managerial duties.

After four months at Parkhead, Macari returned to the Potteries to resume charge of Stoke. He remained with the club until 1997 when he left to manage Huddersfield Town, but he is now involved in work with the media.

SHAUN MALONEY

Born: Mirri, Malaysia, 24 January 1983
Celtic career: 1999 to 2007
Appearances and goals:

League		FA Cup		Lg Cup		Europe	
A	**G**	**A**	**G**	**A**	**G**	**A**	**G**
53/51	26	4/4	0	7/3	8	4/9	1

Total appearances: 68/67
Total goals: 35
League Championships: 2003-04; 2005-06
League Cup: 2005-06
Honours: 2 Scotland caps

Malaysian-born Shaun Maloney is a genuinely exciting talent, quick, inventive and more than capable of serving up the spectacular, yet, nevertheless, there were times during the reign of Martin O'Neill that he failed to convince the then Celtic boss.

Having spent the first four years of his life in Mirri, Malaysia, his family then moved to his mother's home town of Aberdeen, where the young Maloney found a love for sport, particularly football and tennis.

After joining Celtic as a trainee in 1999, Maloney made his first team debut in the 3-0 Old Firm defeat of Rangers at Ibrox Stadium in April 2001. Most of his first team outings over the next couple of seasons were from the bench, but in the 2001-02 League Cup meeting with Stirling Albion, he netted four of Celtic's goals in an 8-0 win.

He looked to be establishing himself as a first team regular in 2003-04, but midway through that campaign he picked up a cruciate ligament injury in an Under-21 match against Partick Thistle. The little striker travelled to the United States to be operated on by Dr Richard Steadman—the man also charged with rescuing John Kennedy's career—and though he eventually made a full recovery, he didn't return to first team action until late on in the following season.

Maloney, who at the time of writing has won two full international caps for Scotland, and could have opted to play for the Republic of Ireland or Malaysia, had an outstanding season in 2005-06, scoring many important goals for the Hoops as they won their 40th League Championship title and League Cup, with Maloney netting one of the goals in the 3-0 defeat of Dunfermline Athletic in the final.

He capped it by winning the SPFA Player of the Year and Young Player of the Year awards, the first time in the awards' 29-year history that a player has won both categories. He also won the Celtic fans' Player of the Year and players' Player of the Year in a season which saw him score 16 goals and contribute with 28 assists.

With his contract expiring at the end of the 2006-07 season, Celtic moved to offer Maloney a new deal. However, they could not agree terms and talks were postponed. Just before the transfer window closed, due to a continuing disagreement over a contract extension, the player, who has incredible stamina and a great eye for goal, signed for Aston Villa for a reported fee of £1 million.

Sadly, injuries have hampered his time at Villa Park, but he is without doubt a huge talent and will surely go on to achieve great things.

STEPHANE MAHE

Born: Puteaux, France, 23 September 1968
Celtic career: 1997 to 2001
Appearances and goals:

League		FA Cup		Lg Cup		Europe	
A	**G**	**A**	**G**	**A**	**G**	**A**	**G**
73/3	4	8	1	9	0	9	0

Total appearances: 99/3

Total goals: 5

League Championships: 1997-98; 2000-01
League Cup: 1997-98; 1999-2000

One of the game's ultimate professionals, defender Stephane Mahe started his career in the AJ Auxerre youth academy, playing alongside Marcel Desailly and Didier Deschamps before graduating to the club's first team under Guy Roux's tutelage in 1989. He suffered a setback in 1992 when involved in a car accident, and from his resulting injuries, was out of the game for over six months. Upon his return the following year, he helped Auxerre to reach the UEFA Cup semi-finals where they lost to Borussia Dortmund. The following year he earned his first winner's medal as Auxerre defeated Montpellier 3-0 in the Coupe de France final.

In 1995 Mahe moved to Paris Saint-Germain, but spent just a single season in the capital, during which PSG won the European Cup Winners' Cup in a match against Rapid Vienna in Brussels. After a season with Stade Rennais, Mahe left France to join Celtic.

Mahe, who joined Celtic on a three-year deal for a fee of around £500,000, had played at Parkhead previously as part of the PSG side which beat the Hoops on their way to lifting the European Cup Winners' Cup, but made his debut in a Celtic shirt in 2-0 win at St Johnstone in August 1997. That season, Mahe helped Celtic win both the League Championship—

thus ending Rangers' tilt at ten-in-a-row—and the League Cup, defeating Dundee United 3-0 in the final. During the course of that season, Mahe scored his first goal for the club in a fourth round Scottish Cup win at Dunfermline Athletic.

Though Mahe normally played at left-back, his versatility was such that he could play at both wing-back or centre-half, and so was able to be selected in the same team as Hoops' skipper Tommy Boyd.

Mahe, who didn't get on the scoresheet in the league in three of his four seasons with the club, netted four goals during the 1999-2000 season as Celtic finished runners-up to Rangers, including two goals in successive games. That season he was also a member of the Celtic side that again lifted the League Cup, this time beating Aberdeen 2-0.

Mahe sadly fell out of favour under Hoops' boss Martin O'Neill and duly made the short journey along the M8 to pursue his career with Hearts. At Tynecastle, his experience proved invaluable as the Hearts boss Craig Levein had to rely heavily on a number of youngsters. However, a long-standing Achilles injury forced his departure from the Jambos in the summer of 2003.

Mahe returned to his native France, and since August 2003 has worked as manager of lower-league side Saint-Nazaire.

GORDON MARSHALL

Born: Edinburgh, 19 April 1964
Celtic career: 1991 to 1998
Appearances and goals:

League		FA Cup		Lg Cup		Europe	
A	G	A	G	A	G	A	G
100	0	4	0	4	0	4	0

Total appearances: 112
Total goals: 0
Honours: 1 Scotland cap

Gordon Marshall was clearly born to be a goalkeeper. His father, a Parkhead reserve also named Gordon, played just one competitive game for the Hoops, a European Cup match in 1971, before moving on to Aberdeen and then Arbroath. Son Gordon would make his debut in Celtic colours exactly 20 years later, having been bought—also as a reserve—by then manager Liam Brady.

A game against Airdrie was his one and only appearance that term, when first-choice keeper Republic of Ireland international Packie Bonner was injured. The next season he made 16 appearances to Bonner's 20, and when Tommy Burns took the hot seat Marshall made his move and became an ever-present.

Marshall had started his career at Ibrox, but a broken leg while playing for the reserves scuppered hopes of first-team football on that side of Glasgow. After a loan spell with East Stirling, he joined East Fife. Proving to be one of Scotland's best young keepers, he moved on to Falkirk, and in 1990-91 helped the Bairns win the First Division Championship. His form alerted Glasgow's two big clubs—Rangers wanted him back as an understudy to Andy Goram, but he opted to join the Hoops.

Liam Brady invested £275,000 on the advice of his assistant Tommy Craig, realising the importance of having two good goalkeepers. And if the central defenders immediately in front of him, Boyd and Hughes, had helped Celtic boast the best defensive record in the Scottish Premier Division, Marshall had also contributed with numerous shut-outs. His consistency, sure handling ability, quick shot-stopping reflexes and sound positional sense would surely have made him an international regular, had it not been for the dependable duo of Leighton and Goram ahead of him in the pecking order.

Marshall's only game at full international level came when Andy Roxburgh selected him for the match against the United States at the Mile High Stadium in Denver. In a difficult game, Marshall kept a clean sheet as Scotland won 1-0.

Tommy Burns' final season at the helm saw him pick Stuart Kerr from the outset, but Marshall found his way back to first team action later in the season when the youngster dislocated a finger.

Marshall eventually left the Hoops, after appearing in exactly 100 league games, to join Kilmarnock for a fee of £150,000. He missed very few games in his stay at Rugby Park, and in 2000-01 helped the club reach the League Cup Final where they lost 3-0 to Celtic! In the summer of 2003, Marshall joined Motherwell, where his form was nothing short of outstanding, but having reached the ripe old age of 41, he lost his place to Graeme Smith and took up a coaching position with Hibernian.

FRANK McAVENNIE

Born: Glasgow, 22 November 1959
Celtic career: 1987 to 1989 and 1992 to 1993
Appearances and goals:

League		FA Cup		Lg Cup		Europe	
A	G	A	G	A	G	A	G
82/3	37	10	4	7	8	4	1

Total appearances: 103/3
Total goals: 50
League Championships: 1987-88
Scottish Cup: 1987-88
Honours: 5 Scotland caps

Frank McAvennie tasted the highs and lows of Scottish football in equal measure during a turbulent first spell of two years at Parkhead, which saw him summoned to court following an Old Firm bust-up just 15 days into his Celtic career!

He started out with St Mirren, where he demonstrated brilliant heading ability and an explosive shot before being snapped up by West Ham United for a fee of £340,000 in the summer of 1985. A relatively unknown player when he arrived at Upton Park, no-one could have anticipated the impact he made on the English First Division, leading to him winning full international recognition for Scotland, and he scored on his debut in the World Cup qualifying game against Australia. In 1985-86, McAvennie topped the club's goalscoring charts with 26 league goals, a figure only bettered by Gary Lineker. After an indifferent season in 1986-87 and a poor start to the following campaign, Celtic came in with a record bid of £750,000 which neither player nor club could refuse.

Macca, a prolific goalscorer often likened to Denis Law, will always be remembered for his part in the Ibrox fracas of 15 October 1987. Along with Rangers pair Chris Woods and Terry Butcher, McAvennie was shown the red card after a goalmouth scuffle, which ended with the Ibrox men being charged with disorderly conduct and fined £500 and £250 respectively. As expected, McAvennie was found not guilty. The verdict appeared to lift a huge burden from his shoulders and allowed him to resume his prolific goalscoring partnership with Andy Walker, which helped deliver the League and Cup double later that year.

In fact, it was McAvennie who carved a niche for himself in the club's history books when scoring both goals in the 2-1 Scottish Cup Final victory over Dundee United, at the end of what was the team's centenary year of 1988.

McAvennie returned to West Ham for personal reasons the following year, much to the annoyance of the Celtic fans, but never recaptured the goalscoring touch which had tempted the Londoners to part with over £1 million. He was unable to prevent the Hammers' relegation to Division Two, and worse was to come when, on the opening day of the 1989-90 season, he broke his leg in the match at Stoke City. He was back to his best the following season, as the club regained its top flight status, later netting a hat-trick against Nottingham Forest in what turned out to be his farewell game.

After unsuccessful short-term spells with Aston Villa, Cliftonville and South China of Hong Kong, he returned to Celtic. McAvennie topped up his Parkhead tally of goals with another nine, before departing for good in February 1993. Several monthly trial periods with Swindon Town, Airdrie, Falkirk and St Mirren were the final stops on his 14-year career, and in 1995 he brought the curtain down on his footballing career, in order to pursue his business interests.

Cleared of a well-publicised drugs charge, he now has a place on the Saturday morning football show, Soccer AM—where the car park is named after him. This was a result of him hitting a Russian substitute, who was warming up at the time for a feature on the programme, in the face with a volley. Since that day, it has been known as the Frank McAvennie Car Park!

JOE McBRIDE

Born: Govan, 10 June 1938
Celtic career: 1965 to 1968
Appearances and goals:

League		FA Cup		Lg Cup		Europe	
A	G	A	G	A	G	A	G
52/3	54	8	3	21	24	10	5

Total appearances: 91/3
Total goals: 86
League Championships: 1965-66; 1966-67
League Cup: 1965-66; 1966-67
Honours: 2 Scotland caps

The bustling, energetic Joe McBride played only three seasons for Celtic, whereas he had played another 13 for the following clubs—Kilmarnock, Wolves, Luton Town, Partick Thistle, Motherwell, Hibernian, Dunfermline Athletic and Clyde. Yet he is best remembered as Joe McBride of Celtic!

The reason for this was simple. McBride scored goals wherever he went, and indeed had a strike rate of over 90%, but, at Parkhead, he belonged to the most attack-minded and explosive side in the country. McBride was Jock Stein's first-ever signing, costing £22,000 from Motherwell. In his inaugural season with the Hoops, he ended the campaign as the club's top scorer with 31 goals in 30 league games.

Capped twice by Scotland against Wales and Northern Ireland in the autumn of 1966, he also netted a hat-trick while playing for the Scottish League in a 6-0 victory over the League of Ireland at Parkhead.

In that 1966-67 season, McBride had already scored 35 goals in 26 games, when in the Christmas Eve fixture with Aberdeen, his knee gave way. Despite not playing in any further games that season—one in which Celtic won every competition including the European Cup—he remained the country's top-scorer at the season's end.

Sadly for McBride, by the time he had regained match fitness a year later—though it was doubtful whether he was ever fully fit again—events had overtaken him. The Hoops were now a major force in Europe and Jock Stein, a man of unwavering determination once his mind was made up, had evolved a system around a main strike force of Chalmers and Wallace. Joe

Joe McBride playing against Rangers in the League during the 1965-66 season
(www.snspix.com)

McBride as perennial squad player was unthinkable, and in November 1968 he moved on to play for Hibernian as a replacement for Colin Stein.

McBride's primary role was that of a finisher, and, at Easter Road, this player, who could score with either foot and despite his lack of inches was useful in the air, continued to find the net. He finished as Hibs' tops scorer in both 1968-69 and 1969-70. He later played for Dunfermline Athletic before finishing his playing days with Clyde.

The courage, style and obvious relish he took in his performances in the green and white, allied to the cruel way he was robbed of his rightful destiny, won him the undying affection of a generation of Celtic supporters—for whom Joe McBride will always be an honorary Lisbon Lion.

Jock Stein described him as the quintessential striker, a man who stuck the ball in the back of the net when he couldn't think of anything else to do with it, while the great Jimmy McGrory included him at centre-forward without a moment's hesitation in his all-time Celtic XI.

BRIAN McCLAIR

Born: Bellshill, 8 December 1963
Celtic career: 1983 to 1987
Appearances and goals:

League		FA Cup		Lg Cup		Europe	
A	**G**	**A**	**G**	**A**	**G**	**A**	**G**
129/16	99	14/4	11	19/1	9	14/3	3

Total appearances: 176/24
Total goals: 122
League Championships: 1985-86
Scottish Cup: 1984-85
Honours: 30 Scotland caps

Brian McClair will go down in history as one of the most whole-hearted players who have ever played for Celtic.

He was actually on Aston Villa's books as a youngster, but never made it at Villa Park and returned north of the Border to sign for Motherwell. The striker grabbed the headlines in one astonishing week in 1982 when he netted a hat-trick against Rangers and two goals against Celtic for the Fir Park side.

That was more than enough to convince Billy McNeill to sign McClair, and he went on to enjoy a most profitable time at Parkhead, even though, ironically, it would be under McNeill's replacement, David Hay, that 'Choccy' netted 23 goals in 35 league games, bringing an instant return on Celtic's investment. Two goals on the last day of the 1985-86 season helped secure a memorable 5-0 victory over St Mirren which, with once-runaway leaders Hearts capitulating at Dundee, helped give Celtic an unlikely League Championship triumph.

McClair was top scorer for each of his four seasons at Parkhead, netting 35 goals in 1986-87, his final campaign, at the end of which he was voted Scotland's Player of the Year. However, former Aberdeen manager Alex Ferguson knew what McClair could do, and took him to Old Trafford in a hotly contested transfer deal, in which a tribunal eventually awarded the Hoops £850,000.

In his first season at Old Trafford, McClair became the first United player since George Best in 1967-68 to notch up more than 20 Football League goals in a season. McClair's total of 24 included a hat-trick against Derby County. Following the return of Mark Hughes, the player McClair had been signed to replace, the two of them formed a formidable partnership, culminating in United beating Crystal Palace in the 1990 FA Cup Final. The following year the Reds beat Barcelona 2-1 to win the European Cup Winners' Cup and, in 1992, McClair scored the winner in the League Cup Final defeat of Nottingham Forest—appropriately his 100th goal for the Old Trafford club.

During United's 1992-93 Premiership-winning season, McClair switched to midfield, and over the next few seasons, his canny skills and remarkable vision gave the side that extra dimension. A great club man, he went on to earn a deserved testimonial in 1996-97, a season which ended with him winning his fourth Championship medal. After spending most of the following season on the bench, he signed for Motherwell, the club he had started out with.

It soon became apparent that his best years were behind him, as the fast tempo of Scottish football passed him by, and, in December 1998, he became Brian Kidd's assistant at Blackburn Rovers. Unable to prevent their relegation from the Premiership, he was sacked and returned to Old Trafford as youth team coach. In his first season he led the reserve team to the title, while the following season he was in charge of the Under-19 team which clinched the 2003 FA Youth Cup. He has recently been appointed Manchester United's academy director.

GEORGE McCLUSKEY

Born: Hamilton, 19 September 1957
Celtic career: 1974 to 1983
Appearances and goals:

League		FA Cup		Lg Cup		Europe	
A	**G**	**A**	**G**	**A**	**G**	**A**	**G**
121/24	54	16/2	12	26/2	7	11/2	5

Total appearances: 174/30
Total goals: 78
League Championships: 1978-79; 1980-81;
Scottish Cup: 1979-80

If George McCluskey could have found another yard or so of pace, he would have been one of the greatest strikers in the history of Celtic Football Club. Having scored one of the goals for Scotland Schoolboys in their 4-2 win over their English counterparts at Wembley, he certainly looked the part when he burst onto the scene, a product of the Parkhead youth scheme.

He scored on his Celtic debut after coming off the bench against Switzerland's FC Valur in October 1975, before making his league debut against Rangers the following month. He began to score some superb goals, including a 30-yard free-kick against Dundee United in September 1979, the opener against Real Madrid in the European Cup quarter-finals six months later, and the 89th minute strike against Johann Cruyff's Ajax in Amsterdam in September 1982.

McCluskey won his first League Championship medal in 1978-79 when he helped himself to a dozen goals, and the following year he managed to create a bit of history; it was McCluskey's extra-time winner in the Old

Firm Scottish Cup Final which sparked off an on-field riot between rival fans, and, in the aftermath, alcohol was banned from football grounds in Scotland.

McCluskey's career should have blossomed after that, but the emergence of Charlie Nicholas and the prolific goalscoring of Frank McGarvey meant he was left on the bench more often than not. He still managed to score a lot of goals for the Hoops until he left Parkhead for Leeds United in 1983, having decided that manager McNeill preferred the teaming of McGarvey and Nicholas.

His Scotland career never got off the ground, despite being selected by Jock Stein for the Scotland 1982 World Cup squad. When it was trimmed from 40 to the final 22, McCluskey, along with team-mate Tommy Burns, found himself out in the cold. At club level though, his goals helped Celtic to three titles in five seasons.

Having joined Leeds for a fee of £160,000, he lacked consistency during his time at Elland Road and in the summer of 1986 he signed for Hibernian. He later left Easter Road for Hamilton Academical, before, in May 1992, joining Kilmarnock. Within a matter of months he had been appointed Killie's player-coach, but in October 1994 he was transferred to Clyde.

It is unfortunate that a player with such an abundance of skill as George McCluskey could not fulfil his full potential during nearly a decade at Parkhead, though he did enjoy a long career, playing well into his thirties.

FRANK McGARVEY

Born: Glasgow, 17 March 1956
Celtic career: 1980 to 1985
Appearances and goals:

League		FA Cup		Lg Cup		Europe	
A	G	A	G	A	G	A	G
159/9	77	20/4	13	29/6	11	19	8

Total appearances: 227/19
Total goals: 109
League Championships: 1980-81; 1981-82
Scottish Cup: 1979-80; 1984-85
League Cup: 1982-83
Honours: 7 Scotland caps

Frank McGarvey's most famous moment as a Celtic player went hand in hand with his biggest disappointment. The unpredictable striker left Parkhead just days after helping the club to one of its most famous triumphs. McGarvey stooped to head a dramatic late winner, which secured a 2-1 win over Dundee United in the Centenary 1985 Scottish Cup Final. It remains a priceless moment in the memory of many Celtic fans, yet McGarvey's reward was a poor contract offer for the following season and a subsequent £75,000 transfer to St Mirren.

He had started out with St Mirren, but was loaned to Kilsyth Rangers to further his development. On his return to Love Street he soon became a first team regular, scoring 17 times in 1976-77 and helping the club win the Scottish First Division. His form attracted the attention of Bob Paisley, and in May 1979 McGarvey signed for Liverpool for £300,000. However, his tenure with the club lasted less than a year, and, unable to break into the side, he moved to Celtic for £250,000. In doing so, he did for a short time become Scotland's most expensive footballer.

McGarvey accepted a drop in wages to ensure first-team football. His partnership with a vibrant teenager by the name of Charlie Nicholas was feared throughout Scotland, Prince Charlie's sublime skill being complemented by McGarvey's hard work and a flair for the unexpected. It was suggested that McGarvey had no idea what his next move on the pitch would be—making it near impossible for his team-mates, let alone the opposition, to figure it out!

He was a member of the Celtic team that threw the 1980 League title away, but which beat Rangers 1-0 in that season's Scottish Cup Final. He spearheaded the Celtic teams in the Championship-winning seasons of 1980-81 and 1981-82, and won a League Cup winners' badge in 1982 when the Hoops beat Rangers 2-1.

Celtic fans loved his all-or-nothing style, and he rewarded them with a succession of goals and vintage displays. In 1984-85, his last season with the club, he became the first player to score a century of Premier League goals when he converted a hat-trick for Celtic against St Mirren. Yet, amazingly, only days after scoring that Cup Final winner against Dundee United, he had rejoined the Buddies.

Two years after rejoining St Mirren, he won a third Scottish Cup medal, going on to score 125 goals in 387 games before becoming player-manager of Queen of the South. He later joined Clyde and, in 1992-93, was their top scorer with 16 goals as they captured the Second Division Championship. He later ended his career with a spell at Shotts Bon Accord, but having hung up his boots, he now works as a joiner.

AIDEN McGEADY

Born: Glasgow, 4 April 1986
Celtic career: 2004 to 2007
Appearances and goals:

League		FA Cup		Lg Cup		Europe	
A	G	A	G	A	G	A	G
60/29	14	5/5	0	3/3	1	7/3	0

Total appearances: 75/40
Total goals: 15

League Championships: 2005-06; 2006-07
Scottish Cup: 2004-05; 2006-07
Honours: 11 Republic of Ireland caps

For a short spell in his young teens, Aiden McGeady played for amateur club Queen's Park, before the club allowed him to move to the team he supported, Celtic. He was tracked by many top teams both north and south of the Border, with both Alex Ferguson and Liam Brady making personal pleas for the youngster to join Manchester United and Arsenal respectively. Described as the most coveted schoolboy footballer in Britain, he signed a lucrative boot deal with Adidas at the age of only 16.

Described by Martin O'Neill as a player with 'enormous potential', he made his first team breakthrough towards the end of the 2003-04 season. Not only did he score on his debut in a 1-1 draw against Hearts, but he was named Man of the Match.

As a young player, McGeady represented the Scottish Schoolboys national team until he joined Celtic. At that time the SFA policy, incompatible with the policy at Celtic which does not allow such arrangements, was that a player had to be registered with a schoolboys team in order to represent Scottish Schoolboys. Packie Bonner, who knew of his Irish lineage—his paternal grandfather was Irish—invited McGeady to play for the Irish Schoolboys team (who, unlike the SFA, do not insist on schoolboys actually playing for their school team). Since then he has played for a number of Irish sides prior to making his full international debut against Jamaica in June 2004.

An attack-minded midfielder who likes to operate either in the hole behind the strikers or out wide on either wing, McGeady was offered a four-year contract prior to the start of the 2004-05 season. This campaign proved to be the making of young McGeady, as he justified Martin O'Neill's faith in him. He netted five goals in 37 games, including one in the 6-0 demolition of Dunfermline Athletic, and came off the bench to replace Alan Thompson in the 1-0 Scottish Cup Final win over Dundee United.

A player of prodigious talent—full of flicks, tricks and subtle touches—he was voted Celtic's Young Player of the Year in 2004-05, and he repeated the achievement the following season when he helped the Hoops win the Scottish Premier League Championship. His form under new manager Gordon Strachan has been nothing short of outstanding, and in 2006-07 he helped the Parkhead club retain the title and Scottish Cup, defeating Dunfermline Athletic.

Though his decision to opt for the Republic of Ireland instead of his country of birth has been the subject of some controversy in Scotland, and left many Scots disappointed with the player's choice of national team, McGeady himself explains it as loyalty to the team that picked him as an unknown youngster.

Celtic: 100 Heroes   **95**

MARK McGHEE

Born: Glasgow, 20 May 1957
Celtic career: 1985 to 1989
Appearances and goals:

League		FA Cup		Lg Cup		Europe	
A	**G**	**A**	**G**	**A**	**G**	**A**	**G**
82/5	27	12/3	4	4	1	6/1	2

Total appearances: 104/9
Total goals: 34
League Championships: 1985-86; 1987-88
Scottish Cup: 1987-88; 1988-89
Honours: 4 Scotland caps

When Mark McGhee joined the Hoops from German side Hamburg SV in November 1985, he was not totally welcome at Parkhead, being regarded, along with Gordon Strachan, as responsible for getting Roy Aitken ordered off in the Scottish Cup Final of 1984.

The burly striker joined Bristol City as a youngster before returning north of the border with Morton in 1975. His performances at Cappielow Park attracted the attention of several sides, including Newcastle United, who signed him at the tail end of 1977 for a fee of £150,000. He never really settled at St James Park, and, in March 1979, he was snapped up by Aberdeen for just over half of what the Magpies had paid for him.

In his first season at Pittodrie, he helped the Dons win the League Championship as he developed into an unorthodox goalpoacher. The highlight of McGhee's stay with Aberdeen came in 1982-83, when his cross was met by John Hewitt for the dramatic European Cup Winners' Cup Final winner. The following year, his last with the Dons, he helped them defeat Hamburg to lift the Super Cup. Little did he know that he was playing against his next employers. A second League Championship medal was added to his collection, before he scored the extra-time winner against Celtic to win the 1984 Scottish Cup for the Pittodrie club!

McGhee spent a year and a half in Germany before coming back to Scotland with Celtic. He made his debut in an Old Firm match against Rangers which the Light Blues won 3-0, but soon settled into the side, helping them win the League title in his first season with the club. Able to hold the ball up, link well and finish with deadly accuracy from the tightest of chances, he endeared himself to Celtic fans in the Scottish Cup semi-final of 1988 against Hearts. The Jambos were leading 1-0 with just a couple of minutes to go, when McGhee, who had just come off the bench, threaded a glorious equaliser through a packed defence. Then, right on time, he set up Andy Walker for the winner in one of the most delirious finishes ever seen at Hampden Park.

In October 1988 McGhee was credited with scoring Celtic's 999th Premier

League goal—also against Hearts—later captaining the side to victory over Liverpool in the Dubai Super Cup.

On leaving Parkhead, he had another spell with Newcastle before being appointed player-manager of Reading. He took the Royals to the Second Division Championship in 1993-94, before moving to take charge at Leicester City. Citing lack of ambition at the East Midlands club, he left to manage Wolverhampton Wanderers, but eventually paid the price for the club's lack of success. He then managed Millwall, and, in 2000-01, his first season at the club, led them to the Second Division Championship. He recently managed Brighton and Hove Albion, helping the Seagulls gain promotion to the Football League Championship in his season on the south coast. However, after a poor start to the 2006-07 season, McGhee lost his job, and though he was linked to the vacant managerial post at Bohemians, he was, in the summer of 2007, appointed manager of Motherwell.

DANNY McGRAIN

Born: Finnieston, 1 May 1950
Celtic career: 1967 to 1987
Appearances and goals:

League		FA Cup		Lg Cup		Europe	
A	**G**	**A**	**G**	**A**	**G**	**A**	**G**
433/8	4	60	1	105/1	3	53/1	0

Total appearances: 651/10

Total goals: 8

League Championships: 1972-73; 1973-74; 1976-77; 1978-79; 1981-82; 1985-86
Scottish Cup: 1973-74; 1974-75; 1976-77; 1979-80; 1984-85
League Cup: 1974-75; 1982-83
Honours: 62 Scotland caps

Assistant-manager Sean Fallon spotted a young Danny McGrain playing for Scotland schoolboys in 1967, and one look was all he needed to be convinced he had a future star on his hands. Danny McGrain, often to be found at Ibrox as a schoolboy (although he insists he was never a real Rangers supporter) was the mainstay of Jock Stein's Quality Street Kids.

He had had spells with Drumchapel Amateurs and Queen's Park Victoria before Celtic signed him and farmed him out to Maryhill Harps for six months. He then bided his time with the Hoops' successful second string, before making a brief appearance from the bench in a midweek League Cup tie at Dundee United. His league debut came on 29 August 1970 in a 2-0 home win over Morton.

McGrain was no stranger to serious injury or illness. In 1972 he fractured his skull playing against Falkirk at Brockville, and five years later picked up a foot injury against Hibernian which was so serious it kept him out of

Danny McGrain proudly holding the League Championship trophy for the 1985-86 season (www.snspix.com)

the first team for 18 months. In between, in 1974, like the author, he was diagnosed as having diabetes—an illness he insisted would not prevent him plying his trade at the very highest level.

McGrain's career was embroidered with glittering success. With Celtic he won every domestic honour, including six League Championships, five Scottish Cups and two League Cups as well as becoming the club's most capped player. Jock Stein, with typical wry humour, always insisted, 'He's a brilliant full-back with one weakness—he doesn't score enough goals!'

McGrain, who won the first of his 62 caps for Scotland against Wales in 1973, was one of the players who could take great credit for making Scotland a force to be reckoned with again after the 1974 World Cup Finals, where he had played a heroic part in Scotland's goalless draw against Brazil. A serious foot injury ruled him out of the 1978 trip to Argentina, but once again he showed his resilience by bouncing back to reclaim his place in the 1982 World Cup with distinction.

McGrain, who was the key figure in Celtic's double-winning side of 1976-77, capped a wonderful season by being nominated the Football Writers' Player of the Year and helping Scotland defeat England at Wembley.

He was granted a testimonial against Manchester United in 1980, and when his glittering career ended seven years later, fans fully expected his 20 years of dedication to the club to result in a back-room post being offered.

But the silence from the boardroom was deafening, and McGrain, who was awarded the MBE for services to football in 1983, was allowed to leave to join Hamilton Academical, where he won a First Division Championship medal. He later became coach at Clydebank before being appointed manager of Arbroath. Here he became something of a cult figure with many of the club's supporters, who would wear false moustaches and beards at games in his honour.

Following a spell working in corporate entertainment at the Gleneagles golf course, Danny McGrain, whose story is as much a tribute to his character as his ability, is back at Celtic as assistant-trainer to the club's reserve side.

DUNCAN MACKAY

Born: Springburn, 14 July 1937
Celtic career: 1955 to 1964
Appearances and goals:

League		FA Cup		Lg Cup		Europe	
A	G	A	G	A	G	A	G
162	5	33	2	37	0	4	0

Total appearances: 236
Total goals: 7
Honours: 14 Scotland caps

A stylish right-back considered by many to be years ahead of his time, Dunky Mackay played nine seasons at Parkhead during the unsuccessful era of the so-called 'Kelly Kids'.

He had played his early football with St Mary's Boys' Guild and Maryhill Harp, before arriving at Parkhead with Bertie Auld in April 1955. His first few seasons with the club saw him play as a wing-half in the club's reserve side, but he made his Celtic debut at right-back as a replacement for the injured Sean Fallon in the match against Clyde in August 1958.

Within weeks, he was being hailed as the discovery of the season, and towards the end of his first season, he was stepping out for Scotland behind skipper Bobby Evans at Wembley. Though England won 1-0, MacKay had a fine game, with Bolton winger Dougie Holden barely getting a look in.

MacKay was one of the pioneers of the overlapping full-back role, utilising his great speed to advantage. He always tried to play himself out of trouble, refusing to clear the ball in a hurry.

Within 18 months of making his debut, he had been appointed Celtic's captain and led them in two Cup Finals against Dunfermline Athletic. Shortly after this, he decided he wanted to cash in on his speed and skill and join the exodus of Scottish talent moving south to the Football League. Though Johnny Carey came a number of times to Parkhead to watch him, no English club made a firm offer for his services, and he remained with the Hoops.

He lost the captaincy to Billy McNeill in August 1963, and then, a couple of months later, his right-back spot to Ian Young. Sadly, his only honours while with Celtic were two appearances in losing Scottish Cup Finals, although his skills were recognised with frequent selection for the national side.

Having scored seven goals in 236 games, he left the Hoops to join Bobby Evans at Third Lanark just months before Jock Stein took over the reins at Parkhead.

After a season with Third Lanark, he emigrated to Australia when he was appointed player-coach of the Melbourne-based side, Croatia FC. He returned to Scotland in 1972, coaching the junior outfit St Anthony's, while working as a manager of a Glasgow manufacturing firm. He subsequently returned to Australia to become player-coach at Azzurri FC in Perth, and Essendon Lions in Melbourne.

TOSH McKINLAY

Born: Glasgow, 3 December 1964
Celtic career: 1994 to 1999
Appearances and goals:

League		FA Cup		Lg Cup		Europe	
A	**G**	**A**	**G**	**A**	**G**	**A**	**G**
85/14	0	17/1	0	6/2	0	11/1	0

Total appearances: 119/18
Total goals: 0
Scottish Cup: 1994-95
Honours: 22 Scotland caps

Though he was a huge Celtic fan as a boy, Glasgow-born full-back Tosh McKinlay started out with Dundee, signing for the Dens Park club from Celtic Boys Club in the summer of 1981.

He was a virtual ever-present during his six-and-a-half seasons with the Dark Blues, but, during that time, they failed to win any domestic honours and it came as no surprise that after making 204 League and Cup appearances, he was transferred to Heart of Midlothian just before Christmas 1988.

Over the next few seasons, McKinlay was one of the Jambo's most consistent performers, and, though he appeared in both full-back positions, few wingers ever got the better of him. In 1991-92 he helped the Tynecastle club finish runners-up to Rangers in the Premier League. His consistency for Hearts led to interest from a number of clubs south of the Border, but when he did eventually part company with the Edinburgh side after appearing in 241 games, it was Celtic manager Tommy Burns who splashed out £350,000 to take him to Parkhead in November 1994.

McKinlay made his Celtic debut in a 2-2 draw at Dundee United, going on to win a Scottish Cup winners medal in his first season with the club after the Hoops had beaten Airdrie 1-0 in the final.

His displays around this time earned McKinlay, who had played for Scotland at Under-21 and 'B' international level, the first of 22 full caps for the national side when, in August 1995, he helped Scotland beat Greece 1-0. Sadly, injuries then hampered his progress at Parkhead, although he had recovered to play in most of the matches in 1996-97 when the Hoops finished runners-up to arch-rivals Rangers in the SPL.

After starting the following League Championship-winning season as the club's first-choice left-back, he lost his place to Stephane Mahe and was languishing in the reserves when given the chance to join Stoke City on loan.

McKinlay was sent off on his Potters debut and was subsequently suspended for three games. But just as his suspension was starting, he was recalled to the Celtic squad. He appeared on a more regular basis in 1998-99, helping the side once again to finish as runners-up. He had played in the club's Scottish Cup semi-final success, but lost out in the final when the Hoops went down to Rangers.

In the summer of 1999 he was allowed to leave Parkhead and joined Kilmarnock. After seeing out his career at Rugby Park, Tosh McKinlay now works as a football agent.

MURDO MACLEOD

Born: Glasgow, 24 September 1958
Celtic career: 1978 to 1987
Appearances and goals:

League		FA Cup		Lg Cup		Europe	
A	G	A	G	A	G	A	G
274/7	55	36/2	7	44	13	33	8

Total appearances: 387/9
Total goals: 83

League Championship: 1978-79; 1980-81; 1981-82; 1985-86
Scottish Cup: 1979-80; 1984-85
League Cup: 1982-83
Honours: 20 Scotland caps

Murdo MacLeod was famous for having one of the hardest shots in Scottish football. When he let go one of his trademark left-foot power drives, it used to strike fear into the hearts of both opposition defenders and goalkeepers.

A product of Glasgow Amateurs, he made his mark when making his debut for Dumbarton in 1976, and soon attracted the attention of other clubs, but Celtic were the first to snap him up. He made the perfect start to his Parkhead career when he scored the goal that wrapped up the League title. Celtic needed to beat Rangers to win the 1978-79 Championship and were 2-1 down to their biggest rivals. But backed by a massive home crowd, and despite being down to 10 men, they stormed into a 3-2 lead before 'Rhino', as he was nicknamed, unleashed a typically unstoppable 30-yard drive that smashed into the net in the final minute.

He was the driving force behind everything Celtic accomplished in the 1980s, although in 1983 his name was linked with a possible move to Rangers.

Murdo MacLeod rifles home Celtic's second goal in a 3-0 victory over Rapid Vienna in the second round of the 1984 European Cup Winners' Cup (www.snspix.com)

Macleod re-signed just as manager Billy McNeill was on the brink of leaving Parkhead. During the first-half of the decade, Macleod helped the Hoops win the Scottish Cup in 1980 and 1985, the League Cup in the autumn of 1982 and League titles in 1980-81, 1981-82 and 1985-86.

The first of 20 Scottish caps came when he was brought on at Hampden in the 1985 Home International match against England, replacing current Celtic boss Gordon Strachan. His big-match experience served him well as Scotland ran out single-goal winners.

MacLeod stayed nine seasons at Parkhead, scoring 83 goals in 396 games before broadening his horizons with a move to Borussia Dortmund in 1987. MacLeod fitted into the German lifestyle and was a hugely popular player among the Dortmund fans. He also did his best from time to time as a pundit for German television.

Having starred for Scotland in the World Cup Finals of Italia '90, he returned to Scotland with Hibernian as player-coach, winning a Skol Cup winners' medal with the Easter Road club. After three years with the Edinburgh club, he moved to Dumbarton as player-coach, later venturing into management with the club. He guided them to promotion to Division One before accepting the post of Partick Thistle manager, but was fired after two seasons at Firhill.

He then returned to Parkhead and was Wim Jansen's assistant during the successful League Championship-winning season of 1997-98. MacLeod now runs a restaurant, and as well as writing for the *Daily Record*, works as a football commentator for BBC Scotland.

STEPHEN McMANUS

Born: Lanark, 10 September 1982
Celtic career: 2003 to 2007
Appearances and goals:

League		FA Cup		Lg Cup		Europe	
A	**G**	**A**	**G**	**A**	**G**	**A**	**G**
80	10	5	0	6	1	9/1	1

Total appearances: 100/1
Total goals: 12
League Championships: 2005-06; 2006-07
Scottish Cup: 2006-07
League Cup: 2005-06
Honours: 8 Scotland caps

Stephen McManus is an uncompromising left-sided centre-back and one of the successes of the club's 2005-06 campaign.

A product of the club's youth academy, he made his debut for the Hoops in a 4-0 win at Hibernian towards the end of the 2003-04 season, going on to play a further four times for Martin O'Neill's side as they wrestled the League title from Rangers.

McManus, who had made appearances for Scotland at Under-16 and Under-18 level, appeared in just two league games the following season, and with competition for defensive starting slots at Parkhead fierce, he was forced to wait for his chance.

That chance came in 2005-06, when he was an ever-present in the side that won both the League Championship and the League Cup, beating Dunfermline Athletic 3-0 in a one-sided final. With manager Gordon Strachan showing considerable faith in him, McManus went from strength to strength, his tough tackling in defence being matched by surprising ability going forward, and he ended the league campaign with seven goals. Probably his best display came on New Year's Day 2006, when he netted two of Celtic's goals in a 3-2 win at Heart of Midlothian.

Nicknamed 'Mick' after the celebrity wrestler who shared the same name, McManus picked up 10 yellow cards over the course of that campaign, demonstrating his ability to play in a variety of positions across the backline—this should, no doubt, ensure a long career in the green and white of the Parkhead club.

McManus was made captain for the first league game of the 2006-07 season, in the match against Kilmarnock, due to regular club captain Neil Lennon being suspended. As the season unfolded, he repeatedly acted as Celtic's vice-captain, though he did receive his marching orders for the first time in his senior career in March 2007 in the match at Falkirk which the Hoops lost 1-0.

He was capped at full international level for Scotland during the early part of the 2006-07 season, coming off the bench to make his debut in the 2-0 defeat by Ukraine. He started the first match of Alex McLeish's reign as international boss, which resulted in a 2-1 win, with Celtic's Craig Beattie hitting a dramatic late winner. He scored his first goal for the national side against Lithuania, acrobatically turning a Shaun Maloney cross into the net.

JACKIE McNAMARA

Born: Glasgow, 24 October 1973
Celtic career: 1995 to 2005
Appearances and goals:

League		FA Cup		Lg Cup		Europe	
A	G	A	G	A	G	A	G
221/16	10	26/5	3	17/2	1	43/9	1

Total appearances: 307/32
Total goals: 15
League Championships: 1997-98; 2000-01; 2001-02; 2003-04

Scottish Cup: 2000-01; 2003-04; 2004-05
League Cup: 1997-98; 1999-2000; 2000-01
Honours: 33 Scotland caps

The son of Celtic and Hibs player Jackie McNamara senior, he suffered a quite horrendous career-threatening injury in March 1989, when, during a training session with Edina Hibs, his right leg was shattered in two places. He fought hard to regain full fitness, and was playing for Gairdoch United when Dunfermline Athletic signed him in September 1991.

In his first season with the Pars, he helped them reach the League Cup Final where they lost 2-0 to Hibs, but a couple of seasons later he helped them finish runners-up in the First Division, a feat they repeated the following season before winning the title in 1995-96.

By that time, McNamara had left East End Park to join Celtic for a fee

Jackie McNamara hurdles the challenge of Rangers' Gavin Rae during a Scottish Cup quarter final in 2004 (www.snspix.com)

of £600,000, and immediately settled in at Parkhead to form an almost telepathic understanding down the right wing with Simon Donnelly. It was their partnership that drove the Hoops to within touching distance of the League Championship, and won for McNamara the Scottish PFA Young Player of the Year award.

He began his Celtic career as an orthodox right-back, before what were seen as apparent defensive limitations saw him converted to the role of right-sided midfielder. He regularly won Player of the Year awards during his first few seasons with the club, and was prominent in the club's title-winning season of 1997-98, a campaign during which they also won the League Cup, beating Dundee United 3-0 in the final. At the end of the season, he was named as the Scottish PFA Player of the Year.

Having won the first of his 33 caps against Latvia in October 1996, McNamara was part of Scotland's squad for the '98 World Cup in France. On his return to Parkhead, he suffered a long run of niggly injuries which then triggered off an ongoing struggle to command a regular place. However, he did come off the bench to replace the injured Lubo Moravcik during the first half of the 2001 Scottish Cup Final at Hampden, and scored the all-important opening goal in a 3-0 win over Hibernian.

Though the arrival of Martin O'Neill saw him relegated to a bit-part reserve role, he did eventually win the former Celtic boss over, and, during the latter part of O'Neill's tenure, was awarded the Footballer Writers' Player of the Year award in 2004. The following year, McNamara was named captain when Paul Lambert was injured. He was awarded a testimonial match against the Republic of Ireland, and new manager Gordon Strachan said that he valued McNamara's presence at the club.

However, McNamara did not feel the contract offered was sufficient, and it was in acrimonious circumstances that he left to join Wolverhampton Wanderers in the summer of 2005 on a free transfer under the Bosman ruling. McNamara's last competitive game for the Hoops was the 2005 Scottish Cup Final, when he captained Celtic to victory over Dundee United.

After a promising start to his Wolves career, McNamara sustained a cruciate knee ligament injury in the game against Leicester City, and it was only in the penultimate game of the season that he returned to first team action. After another season at Molineux when the club reached the Championship play-offs, he left to join Aberdeen on a two-year contract.

BILLY McNEILL

Born: Bellshill, 2 March 1940
Celtic career: 1957 to 1975
Appearances and goals:

League		FA Cup		Lg Cup		Europe	
A	**G**	**A**	**G**	**A**	**G**	**A**	**G**
486	22	94	7	138	4	69	3

Total appearances: 787

Total goals: 36

League Championships: 1965-66; 1966-67; 1967-68; 1968-69; 1969-70; 1970-71; 1971-72; 1972-73; 1973-74
Scottish Cup: 1964-65; 1966-67; 1968-69; 1970-71; 1971-72; 1973-74; 1974-75
League Cup: 1965-66; 1966-67; 1967-68; 1968-69; 1969-70; 1974-75
European Cup: 1966-67
Honours: 29 Scotland caps

A stunning goal by Billy McNeill, one of Celtic's greatest players of all time, in the dying minutes of the 1965 Scottish Cup Final, changed a team of perennial losers into the most successful outfit ever produced in the British Isles. When McNeill rose above the Dunfermline defence to head Charlie Gallagher's 82nd minute corner beyond Jim Herriot, he, according to Jock Stein, who had arrived at Parkhead just two months earlier, showed his team-mates how to win. At the end of the season, he was named the sports writers' Scottish Player of the Year.

Billy McNeill went on to become the most successful captain in the club's history, winning every honour the game had to offer, culminating in European Cup glory over Inter Milan in May 1967. He had already won the first of his paltry 29 caps for Scotland before Stein arrived, but it was after the Big Man took over that the pair changed the face of Scottish football almost overnight.

A dominant figure who commanded his penalty area like a general, 'Caesar' looked every inch a captain, and his aerial prowess, whether in attack—he scored in three Scottish Cup Finals—or defence, made him one of the most feared members of the star-studded Celtic team of the day. However, his nickname was after the actor Cesar Romero rather than the Roman emperor!

His Parkhead career produced nine successive League Championships, seven Scottish Cup winners' medals and six League Cup winners' medals, but surely his biggest moment must have been on that glorious night in Lisbon when he collected the European Cup winners' badge. Having been awarded an MBE in 1974, he finally retired as a footballer after leading the Hoops to a Scottish Cup Final victory over Airdrie in May 1975.

McNeill returned to succeed Stein as manager three years later after spells at Clyde and Aberdeen, leading the Hoops to three Premier Division

Billy McNeill celebrates with team-mates after Celtic won the 1975 Scottish Cup Final, beating Airdrie 3-1 (www.snspix.com)

titles and a Scottish Cup success before being replaced by David Hay after an apparent disagreement with the board.

Unsuccessful spells in charge at Manchester City and Aston Villa followed, before he answered the call to return home to halt the march of the Light Blue army, which was sweeping all before it under the leadership of Graeme Souness.

McNeill again proved he was the man for the big job, delivering the League and Cup double in the club's Centenary Year of 1988 and the Scottish Cup the following year. However, not for the first time, the Parkhead board showed unbelievable short-sightedness in dismissing him after a two-year trophy 'famine', and replacing him with arguably the most unpopular man ever to fill the manager's hot seat, namely Liam Brady.

Many a moon will shine over Parkhead before we see Billy McNeill's like again. He is, quite simply, the greatest Celt of all time.

BILLY McPHAIL

Born: Glasgow, 2 February 1928
Celtic career: 1956 to 1958
Appearances and goals:

League		FA Cup		Lg Cup		Europe	
A	G	A	G	A	G	A	G
33	13	4	4	20	21	-	-

Total appearances: 57
Total goals: 38
League Cup: 1956-57; 1957-58

The younger brother of John McPhail, Billy joined the Hoops just as his big brother retired.

A ladies hairdresser and restaurateur, he once scored five goals for Clyde against Cowdenbeath—four of them headed—but his career with the Bully Wee was blighted by injury. In fact, a knee injury enforced his withdrawal from the club's 1955 Scottish Cup Final side against the Hoops and cost him a winners' medal.

Though Billy McPhail was stylish, elegant and scored goals, Celtic took a huge gamble when, in May 1956, they signed him. His first goal for the club was typical: a header from a Peacock free-kick that rocketed into the back of the East Fife net at Parkhead in the League Cup tie of August 1956. With his two goals against his former club two months later, Celtic won their way into uncharted territory—a League Cup Final. They had to play Partick Thistle twice in the final, but won their most elusive trophy 3-0, with the first two goals netted by Billy McPhail.

After touring the United States in the summer of 1957, he lined up alongside Sammy Wilson as his inside-left partner for the first time in the League Cup game against Hibernian. Both players scored, and it appeared that McPhail had found his perfect foil. When the Hoops won 3-2 at Ibrox to record their first victory on that ground in 22 years, again both players found the net.

Billy McPhail then carved out a special niche for himself in Celtic's history by scoring a hat-trick in the never-to-be-forgotten 7-1 rout of arch-rivals Rangers in that season's League Cup Final. The last of his three goals, scored in the 53rd, 67th and 80th minutes, caused an eruption of trouble at the Rangers end of Hampden Park, with bottle-throwing forcing terrified spectators to seek the sanctuary of the pitch.

In fact, the menace of this darting, elusive centre-forward is best summed up in this description of him completing his tormenting of Rangers centre-half John Valentine when netting that third goal, Celtic's sixth. 'The ball soared into the Ibrox half. Up went McPhail and Valentine. Once again, McPhail, the player with the most elegant head in Scotland, beat his rival to the jump. As Valentine floundered, McPhail darted round him and got the ball from his own header. Away he raced... all on his own. On and on and on. Niven came dashing out of his goal to avert disaster. But before he could do a thing, Billy McPhail coolly tapped the ball past him.'

A knee injury ended his career after only two years at Parkhead, and robbed him of his only international cap after he had been selected to play against Wales. He was expected to make a difference and he did.

JOHN McPHAIL

Born: Lambhill, 27 December 1923
Died: 6 November 2000
Celtic career: 1941 to 1956
Appearances and goals:

League		FA Cup		Lg Cup		Europe	
A	G	A	G	A	G	A	G
141	55	23	17	37	17	-	-

Total appearances: 201
Total goals: 89
League Championships: 1953-54
Scottish Cup: 1950-51
Honours: 5 Scotland caps

One of the most popular figures of his era with the Celtic supporters, big John McPhail was signed from the now defunct Strathclyde Juniors in 1941. His greatest asset was his versatility and he could, and did, play in almost every position. His career was hampered by injuries, however, and, at one point early in his career, he was sent to Ireland to recover from tuberculosis.

Although he began his Parkhead career as a right-half where his strength in the tackle was put to best use, he was soon switched to centre-forward in 1950 and became a remarkable success in his new role. He netted with frequent regularity and was an excellent leader on the park, having been appointed captain in the summer of 1948.

Nicknamed 'Hookey' due to the extraordinary way he was able to control and cross the ball with his right foot, McPhail was a major figure in taking Celtic to their first Scottish Cup triumph for 14 years in 1951, scoring seven of their 19 cup goals despite missing two rounds through injury. His finest hour was the final itself against Motherwell where he scored a memorable winner after just 12 minutes, tearing through the centre of the Steelmen's defence before lifting the ball over the stranded keeper.

He scored on his international debut against Wales at a fogbound Hampden Park in November 1949, as Scotland went on to win 2-0; he also netted twice in the opening minutes of his third international appearance as Northern Ireland were beaten 6-1. A few weeks after this, he produced the only goal of the game that saw the Scottish League defeat the Football League 1-0 at Ibrox.

Later in his career, he began to be troubled by weight problems, and he was sent to a health farm in Tring to diet off the excess. Unable to lose the weight, he was reluctant to play in midfield, but he did lead the attack in the Scottish Cup Final against Clyde in April 1955, a match that ended all-square at 1-1. He was left out of the side for the replay and, thereafter, his first team appearances grew fewer.

Also known as 'Mc "Never" Phail', he decided to retire in 1956 just as his younger brother Billy signed from Clyde.

A sports journalist for a good number of years with the *Daily Record* and the *Celtic View*, John McPhail, who died in November 2000, was a mainstay of the Celtic team for over a decade.

PAUL McSTAY

Born: Hamilton, 22 October 1964
Celtic career: 1982 to 1997
Appearances and goals:

League		FA Cup		Lg Cup		Europe	
A	G	A	G	A	G	A	G
509/6	57	66	6	54	7	43	2

Total appearances: 672/6
Total goals: 72
League Championships: 1985-86; 1987-88;
Scottish Cup: 1984-85; 1987-88; 1988-89; 1994-95
League Cup: 1982-83
Honours: 76 Scotland caps

Few who saw Paul McStay orchestrate Scotland schoolboys' 5-4 victory over England at Wembley in 1980 could have doubted that a glittering career at the highest level lay ahead for this most modest of young men. McStay was a gifted midfielder with superb close control and pin-point distribution. He made his debut as a 17-year-old, marking his first full game in the green

Paul McStay on the attack during the 1988 Scottish Cup Final, which Celtic went on to win, beating Dundee United 2-1 (www.snspix.com)

and white with a goal against Aberdeen in a 3-1 win at Pittodrie. Later that year he was part of the Scotland side which won the European Under-18 Championship.

McStay, who joined the Hoops from Parkhead Boys' Club in February 1981, was only 18 when he earned his first full cap for Scotland in a 2-0 victory over Uruguay at Hampden.

After an excellent 1982-83 campaign he was voted the Scottish PFA Young Player of the Year. He was a major factor behind the club winning the double in its Centenary Year and collected both the Scottish Football Writers' and Players' Player of the Year awards in 1988. In the 1989 Scottish Cup Final against Rangers, he was head and shoulders above the rest in a 1-0 win.

In January 1990 he followed his great uncles, Willie and Jimmy McStay, by becoming the third member of the family to captain Celtic, when the previous incumbent Roy Aitken was transferred to Newcastle United.

Sadly, his tenure as skipper coincided with Rangers' domination of the domestic scene in Scotland, and the Scottish Cup victory over Airdrie in 1995 was his only moment of glory while leading the Parkhead club.

A one-club man who shunned lucrative offers from top English and European clubs, McStay won two League Championships, one League Cup and four Scottish Cup medals in a career which saw him turn out in 678 games for the Hoops. Labelled 'unquestionably the best player in Scotland in the late 1980s' by team-mate Tommy Burns, McStay represented the national side 76 times—the last as a substitute against Austria at Parkhead in April 1997.

Awarded the MBE for his services to football in the 1997 New Years' Honours List, McStay, who was rewarded for his loyalty by Celtic with a lucrative testimonial against Manchester United in 1995, was forced to quit the game due to a persistent ankle injury in the summer of 1997.

In 2002 he was voted a member of Celtic's greatest-ever team by the club's fans. He is also a member of the Scotland Football Hall of Fame.

A quiet, modest family man who never made an enemy on or off the pitch during his glittering 16-year stay at Parkhead, Paul McStay must surely be acknowledged as one of Celtic's all-time greats.

JOE MILLER

Born: Glasgow, 8 December 1967
Celtic career: 1987 to 1993
Appearances and goals:

League		FA Cup		Lg Cup		Europe	
A	G	A	G	A	G	A	G
113/39	28	19/2	2	10/3	2	8/1	1

Total appearances: 150/45
Total goals: 33
League Championships: 1987-88
Scottish Cup: 1987-88; 1988-89

Having started his career with Aberdeen in 1985, midfielder Joe Miller joined Celtic in November 1987, and, at the age of 19, made a goalscoring debut in a 5-0 home win over Dundee.

In his first season with the Hoops, Miller went on to help the club win both the League Championship and Scottish Cup, beating Dundee United 2-1. Initially though, he was employed by both Billy McNeill and his successor Liam Brady as a winger, a position he never occupied during his time at Pittodrie. Sadly, he was tried through the middle even during periods of goal drought, when the club's predicament called out for some experiment.

Joe Miller earned immortality towards the end of the first half of the club's 1989 Scottish Cup Final appearance against Rangers, when he stole Gary Stevens' back-pass and drilled home the winner past England international keeper Chris Woods. Only weeks before that big game, the Hoops had trailed 2-1 to their great rivals in the League when they were awarded a penalty. Miller insisted he would take it. Woods managed to parry the shot and the onrushing Miller put the ball well over the bar!

There is little doubt that Miller's greatest game in the green and white of Celtic was another Scottish Cup tie against the Light Blues on St Patrick's Day 1991. He was outstanding, pulling all the strings in a 2-0 win for the Hoops.

In the summer of 1993, Miller rejoined the Dons, having been sold to part-finance the purchase of Hibs' midfielder Pat McGinlay.

In his first season in his second spell at Pittodrie, Miller was instrumental in the club finishing as runners-up to Rangers, and he enjoyed a further five seasons with the club, taking his total of league games, in which he scored 32 goals, to 209. In 1998, Miller moved on to Dundee United, though he was troubled by a spate of niggling injuries during his two years at Tannadice.

He spent a season in the Australian NSL playing for Parramatta Power, and also helped North Sydney Soccer Club to win the KDSA Grand Final in 2003.

He later returned to Scotland, and, after brief spells with Raith Rovers and Clydebank, joined Clyde as assistant-manager to Graham Roberts. In 2006, Miller was appointed the club's manager after the departure of Roberts following a feud between the pair. He later took Clyde to the Challenge Cup Final, the club's first national final in over 40 years.

WILLIE MILLER

Born: Glasgow, 20 November 1924
Died: 19 June 2005
Celtic career: 1942 to 1950
Appearances and goals:

League		FA Cup		Lg Cup		Europe	
A	**G**	**A**	**G**	**A**	**G**	**A**	**G**
94	0	6	0	23	0	-	-

Total appearances: 123
Total goals: 0
Honours: 6 Scotland caps

Unfortunately for goalkeeper Willie Miller, he was at his best when his team, Celtic, were at their worst!

He had started out with the boys' club St Rollox United, before signing for the Hoops from Maryhill Harps in the summer of 1942. At the time, Miller was training to be an engineer on the railways, so he worked throughout the day before going to Parkhead to train at night. Over the next eight years, he proved himself to be a brilliant keeper, equally adept at high and low shots and superb in anticipation and clean handling.

His bravery was never in doubt. In the Inter-League match in March 1947, Miller was concussed and had his nose broken in two places as he prevented Kippax's second goal! He went off, but within a couple of minutes he returned to a tremendous Hampden roar. Thankfully he had recovered in time to play in his second international match for Scotland against England at Wembley the following month.

He was unlucky in that recognition at this level was delayed because of Bobby Brown's prowess in the Scotland goal, and then he was denied further opportunities by the emergence of Jimmy Cowan. In that game against the Auld Enemy, Miller suffered a severe head injury, but time after time his blood-bandaged head was thrown back as his body arched backwards to tip over yet another English volley in a 1-1 draw.

Back at Parkhead, Miller quite often held out alone against team after team, while the defence in front of him dithered dismally. Miller knew that while playing for the Hoops, everything depended on him. Many was the time that he had to dash off his line and make a save at the feet of an onrushing forward—the number of stitches he had in his scalp being too numerous to count!

However, Miller's form declined, and after one slip too many, he lost his place to Bonnar and was allowed to leave Celtic and join Clyde.

He helped the Bully Wee gain a remarkable amount of silverware during the 1951-52 season— the Glasgow Cup, Charity Cup, Supplementary Cup and the Second Division Championship trophy. After four good years, he moved on to Hibernian, but on being unable to displace Tommy Younger as first-choice keeper, he decided to retire.

One of Celtic's finest custodians, he then decided to go on the road as a whisky rep before becoming owner of a public house in the Townhead area of Glasgow.

JOHAN MJALLBY

Born: Stockholm, 9 February 1971
Celtic career: 1998 to 2004
Appearances and goals:

League		FA Cup		Lg Cup		Europe	
A	G	A	G	A	G	A	G
132/12	13	14/2	0	10	1	26	1

Total appearances: 180/14
Total goals: 15
League Championships: 2000-01; 2001-02; 2003-04
Scottish Cup: 2000-01
League Cup: 1999-2000; 2000-01
Honours: 47 Sweden caps

Swedish international Johan Mjallby joined the Hoops from AIK Solna in November 1998, and made his debut in central defence in the 5-1 demolition of Rangers that season. Just a few months prior to joining the Parkhead club, he had scored in Sweden's 2-1 win over England.

Early on in his sporting career he played both football and tennis, and had the choice to turn professional at both sports. He made the decision to make football his number one sport, and was signed by AIK in 1984 from IK Bele.

He spent the next 14 seasons at AIK Solna and established himself in the side with solid performances as a gritty, tough-tackling midfield player. His performances at the club were noticed, and he soon broke into the Swedish national side. Although in the squad when his club won the League in 1991-92, he refused to accept the gold medal, giving as the reason that he didn't feel as though he had contributed enough! Therefore it was a great day when the AIK lifelong supporter Mjallby got his golden prize in 1998, when he guided the club to the title.

His displays for club and country caught the eye of Celtic boss Jozef Venglos, and, after his impressive debut for the Hoops, he continued to grow to prominence in the role of central defender. The following season, Venglos moved into the role of a scout, with John Barnes coming in as head coach and Kenny Dalglish as Director of Football. Mjallby again took up his midfield role in Barnes' new formation, but following the former Liverpool man's departure, he reverted to defence under Dalglish. It was under Dalglish that he won his first honour as a Celtic player in the League Cup win over Aberdeen.

Martin O'Neill replaced Dalglish, and initially Mjallby didn't feature in his plans, generating rumours that he might be surplus to requirements. Eventually, though, he returned to action and picked up a further three medals as Celtic won the domestic treble in 2000-01. The following season saw him experience his first taste of Champions League football, while another Premier League title was added to his growing medal haul.

The 2002-03 season saw Celtic, with Mjallby a prominent figure, reach the final of the UEFA Cup, where they lost 3-2 after extra-time to Porto. The following season was to be his last at Parkhead, and after struggling with injury throughout the campaign he decided to turn down Celtic's offer of a one-year deal.

Mjallby went to play in Spain's La Liga with newly promoted side Levante UD. However, he was not to enjoy the same level of success as he had in Scotland, and was forced to retire as he eventually succumbed to longstanding injuries picked up throughout his time at Parkhead. After almost a year out of the game he made a comeback and signed once again for his boyhood favourites AIK, but again injuries forced his retirement, and this time it was for good.

NEIL MOCHAN

Born: Larbert, 6 April 1927
Died: 28 August 1994
Celtic career: 1953 to 1960
Appearances and goals:

League		FA Cup		Lg Cup		Europe	
A	**G**	**A**	**G**	**A**	**G**	**A**	**G**
191	81	34	16	43	13	-	-

Total appearances: 268
Total goals: 110
League Championships: 1953-54
Scottish Cup: 1953-54
League Cup: 1956-57; 1957-58
Honours: 3 Scotland caps

Neil Mochan was the type of centre-forward that Celtic lacked for much of the immediate post-war period. He was speedy, direct and strong; and possessing a ferocious shot, certainly had an eye for goal. He is remembered in the annals of Celtic folklore for his unstoppable shot in the 1953 Coronation Cup Final victory over Hibs.

After playing his early football for Dunipace Thistle, he joined Morton in April 1944. His performances for the Cappielow Park club—although

National Service prevented him from playing in the club's epic Scottish Cup Final and replay with Rangers in 1948—led to a number of top clubs showing an interest in his future.

In the summer of 1951, Middlesbrough paid £14,000 to take him to Ayresome Park. Mochan, who played his first game for the Teesside club in the Festival of Britain game against Partizan Belgrade, went on to score 14 goals during 1951-52, but after just one season with Boro, he returned to Scotland to play for Celtic.

Mochan was definitely the inspiration behind the Celtic team that did the League and Cup double in 1953-54. He was the leading League scorer with 20 goals, and netted four on the Hoops' Scottish Cup trail, which culminated in a 2-1 defeat of Aberdeen. In the game against Hibs at Easter Road, Celtic needed two points for the title and came away with a 2-0 win courtesy of two Neil Mochan goals.

Nicknamed 'Smiler', he won the first of his three Scottish caps against Norway in May 1954, and went with Scotland to the World Cup in Switzerland. He was in the side beaten 7-0 in suffocating heat by Uruguay in Basle. Ever the optimist, he sat down at the end of the game and said, 'We could have beaten them!'

He won his first League Cup medal against Partick Thistle in October 1956 and his second a year later in the famous 'Hampden in the sun' game as Celtic hammered Rangers 7-1, with Mochan netting a couple of his side's goals. In February 1960, Mochan scored all five goals in a Scottish Cup tie against St Mirren, yet, towards the end of his Parkhead career, he was surprisingly switched to the left-back berth!

He was transferred to Dundee United, before later ending his playing days with a spell at Raith Rovers. In 1964 he returned to Parkhead as assistant-trainer/coach and became the club's head trainer in the summer of 1965. He prepared the Celtic teams that contested the European Cup Finals of 1967 and 1970, but sadly, this most popular of players took ill during the summer of 1994, and died of leukaemia.

LUBOMIR MORAVCIK

Born: Nitra, Czechoslovakia, 22 June 1965
Celtic career: 1998 to 2002
Appearances and goals:

League		FA Cup		Lg Cup		Europe	
A	G	A	G	A	G	A	G
75/19	29	9/1	1	8/2	2	11/4	3

Total appearances: 103/26
Total goals: 35
League Championships: 2000-01; 2001-02
Scottish Cup: 2000-01

Described by Zinedine Zidane as the best attacking midfielder he had ever seen, Lubomir Moravcik instantly endeared himself to everyone at the Parkhead following his arrival in November 1998.

Having played his early football for Plastika Nitra, a little-known Czechoslovakian side, he forced his way into the national side during the 1990 World Cup qualifying campaign. He proved to be one of the best players on view during Italia '90, but he was sent off in the quarter-final game against West Germany after kicking his boot up in the air after it had come off in a tackle.

That same summer he signed for St Etienne, where he was compared with the brilliant Platini. Voted the best foreign footballer in France's top flight, he also won Czechoslovakia's Player of the Year award in 1992. After spells with Sporting Club de Bastia and the German side MSV Duisburg, Moravcik joined Celtic for a fee of £300,000.

He soon became a hero in the eyes of the Parkhead faithful when, in his first Old Firm encounter, he netted twice in a 5-1 win for the Hoops over their arch-rivals. Sadly, an injury in the game at Motherwell three months later robbed the side of his influential presence.

He was unusual in that he was highly proficient at controlling the ball with both feet, often taking free-kicks and corners with either foot.

The Slovakian was a delight to watch, especially in full flow, and, in April 2001, his two solo goals in the Hoops' 3-0 triumph at Ibrox will long live in the memory of Celtic supporters. He stayed at Parkhead for four seasons, winning two SPL Championships, one Scottish Cup and two CIS Insurance Cups. He bowed out during the 1-1 draw with Rangers in April 2002, but only after receiving a standing ovation from his adoring fans. His testimonial in Slovakia attracted a crowd of over 10,000—five times the average number of spectators—and raised £5,000 for the handicapped children of his home town of Nitra.

On leaving Celtic, he once again joined up with Venglos at Japanese J League team Ichihara, before later being named as Director of Football at SCP Ruzomberok of Slovakia.

CHRIS MORRIS

Born: Newquay, 24 December 1963
Celtic career: 1987 to 1992
Appearances and goals:

League		FA Cup		Lg Cup		Europe	
A	G	A	G	A	G	A	G
157/6	8	22	1	16/1	0	9	0

Total appearances: 204/7
Total goals: 9
League Championships: 1987-88
Scottish Cup: 1987-88; 1988-89
Honours: 35 Republic of Ireland caps

Chris Morris was a natural sportsman, excelling at cricket and rugby as well as football. He looked set for a career as a PE teacher when Sheffield Wednesday manager Jack Charlton signed him for the Owls in October 1982.

Morris broke into the Yorkshire club's league side as a right-winger in 1983-84, but it was only after he switched to full-back that his true potential was revealed. He spent five seasons at Hillsborough before Celtic manager Billy McNeill paid £125,000 to take him to Parkhead in the summer of 1987.

Opting for a formation based around a sweeper and wing-backs, Chris Morris was the perfect choice to assume duties on the Hoops' right flank. He made his debut in a 4-0 win over Morton, his form in his first season at the club leading to him winning his first full cap for the Republic of Ireland—his mother was born in Co. Mayo—in the 5-0 thrashing of Israel.

Looking like Celtic's answer to the loss of Danny McGrain, he helped the Hoops win the double in 1987-88, scoring a goal after just three minutes of the match against Dundee—a game that saw the Centenary Year Championship go to Parkhead.

As for the Republic of Ireland, he could not have timed his entrance on to the international stage any better. The Republic had just clinched a place at their first major tournament finals—the 1988 European Championships—and after five consecutive appearances, he travelled to Euro '88 as the team's first-choice right-back.

He continued his winning ways with Celtic, and, in 1988-89, netted a first-minute goal in the Old Firm game against Rangers, later helping beat the Hoops' greatest rivals to the Scottish Cup.

He had a fine 1990 World Cup for the Republic, and was seen by millions on TV shaking hands with the Romanian players before the penalty shoot-out, which the Irish side went on to win 5-4.

Leaving Celtic to join Middlesbrough in exchange for Andy Payton, Morris damaged a cruciate ligament, and this not only required surgery but kept him out of action for the rest of that season, so ending his chances of playing in the 1994 World Cup. Though he later returned to help Boro win the First Division Championship, Morris was disappointed not to have been offered more opportunities to play in the Premiership, being released at the end of the 1996-97 season.

Chris Morris then ran a pasty restaurant called Morris Pasties in his native Newquay, and has recently branched out and opened a second shop in St Merryn near Padstow.

TONY MOWBRAY

Born: Saltburn, 22 November 1963
Celtic career: 1991 to 1995
Appearances and goals:

League		FA Cup		Lg Cup		Europe	
A	G	A	G	A	G	A	G
75/3	6	5	0	7	0	6	0

Total appearances: 93/3
Total goals: 6

Though he doesn't enjoy the tag, Tony Mowbray can be described as one of the most unfortunate Celtic players in the club's glittering history. The rugged Teessider had built up a reputation as a man-mountain and leader of men during a brilliant 10-year career at Middlesbrough. The Hoops installed Liam Brady as manager for the 1991-92 season, and he immediately pinpointed 'Mogga' as the man to strengthen a weak Parkhead defence.

He was the lynchpin around which the Boro team had been built for more than a decade. A rock at the heart of the Middlesbrough defence, Mowbray stood firm through the liquidation of the club, and was a key figure in the side's resurgence under Bruce Rioch. Mowbray had supported Boro as a boy, and was not only a regular in the team through the 1980s but an inspirational captain. He was part of the Middlesbrough team that climbed into the First Division in 1987-88, and at the end of the following season he was called up into the England 'B' side. He also had the honour of leading Boro out at Wembley in the ZDS Final, but the club's stint in the top flight was short-lived, and, in November 1991, he joined Celtic for £900,000.

The previous month had seen Celtic concede five goals to Swiss team Neuchatel, so Mowbray's arrival was long overdue by anyone's standards.

Mowbray announced on his arrival that he was not flashy, preferring to fight, work, lead and win possession, before allowing Celtic's ball players to take charge. It was a theory which won admiration from the Parkhead faithful, but the reality of Mogga's career in the green and white hoops was somewhat different. Up to then, Mowbray had never suffered serious injury. Within three weeks at Celtic, he was struck down with a troublesome ankle injury which never properly cleared during his four-year stay.

Mowbray also suffered the pain of tragically losing his wife Bernadette to cancer during his time in Glasgow, and his touching story of devotion to her, even after her passing away, won him countless admirers in and out of the game.

Mowbray left Celtic in 1995 in a £350,000 deal which took him to Ipswich Town, where his career was once again to be ravaged by continuing injuries, but by that time his courage and bravery in adversity had made him a never-to-be-forgotten Celt.

In 1998-99 he helped the Suffolk side equal the club record of 26 clean sheets in a season, and although he retained his registration as a player, he was appointed the club's first team coach. He captained Ipswich to the Premiership via the play-offs before turning his attention to coaching.

He later managed Hibernian, making them into a team that consistently challenged at the top of the SPL, before leaving to take over the reins at West Bromwich Albion. He led the Baggies to the play-offs, where they lost 1-0 to Derby in the Wembley final.

BOBBY MURDOCH

Born: Bothwell, 17 August 1944
Died: 15 May 2001
Celtic career: 1959 to 1973
Appearances and goals:

League		FA Cup		Lg Cup		Europe	
A	G	A	G	A	G	A	G
287/4	61	53	13	84	17	54	11

Total appearances: 478/4
Total goals: 102
League Championships: 1965-66; 1966-67; 1967-68; 1968-69; 1969-70; 1970-71; 1971-72; 1972-73
Scottish Cup: 1964-65; 1966-67; 1968-69; 1971-72
League Cup: 1965-66; 1966-67; 1967-68; 1968-69; 1969-70
European Cup: 1966-67
Honours: 12 Scotland caps

More than any other player, Bobby Murdoch benefited from the arrival of Jock Stein, the manager who moulded him into one of the greatest players ever to wear the green and white hoops of Celtic.

Murdoch, who had joined the club straight from school before being 'farmed out' to Cambuslang Rangers, had been at Parkhead six years, having little success as an old-fashioned inside-forward, when Stein, who took over in 1965, moved him alongside Bertie Auld to form the engine room of the 4-2-4 formation which was to fill the Parkhead trophy room to bursting point over the next decade.

The duo, neither of whom could boast the quickest turn of foot, were given the job of forming a seamless link between the rearguard marshalled by Billy McNeill and the fast-paced front pairing of Billy Lennox and Steve Chalmers, a task they took to with consummate ease.

Bobby Murdoch does a lap of honour with his team-mates after Celtic's 6-2 victory over Hibs in the 1972 Scottish Cup Final (www.snspix.com)

In November 1965, Murdoch won the first of his 12 full caps for Scotland in the 1-0 win over Italy. Two of his five goals for the national side came on his next appearance as Wales were defeated 4-1.

Named Scotland's Player of the Year in 1969, he was also a key member of the Lisbon Lions who delivered the European Cup to Parkhead after a 2-1 victory over Inter Milan in May 1967. While Inter Milan coach Helenio Herrera said Murdoch was 'my complete footballer', the scout for Racing Club of Argentina summed up Bobby Murdoch in a more memorable phrase: 'Murdoch—he is Celtic.' And significantly, Celtic's midfielder was limping badly after only a few minutes of the first match of the World Club Championship contest at Hampden Park in 1967.

Murdoch accumulated eight Scottish League Championship medals, four Scottish Cups and five Scottish League Cups.

Jack Charlton described him as 'one of the best players I have ever worked with and certainly the best I've ever signed,' when he took him to Middlesbrough after he had made his final appearance in the hoops of Celtic at the start of the 1973-74 season.

On Teesside, he played a crucial role in steering the north-east club into the First Division. He was thought to have his best days behind him, but he helped Boro cement their place in the top flight before ending his playing days. He stayed at Ayresome Park to coach the club's juniors, but after six years in the backroom staff, Murdoch took over the managerial reins on the departure of John Neal in 1978. The club were relegated, and, after a poor start to the following campaign, his nine-year association with the Teesside club was brought to an end.

Sadly, his health deteriorated in his final years, and prior to his untimely death, he spent his Saturdays as a match day host at Parkhead.

Celtic have always produced cultured midfielders, but none were blessed with the sheer physical presence of Bobby Murdoch, whose successor as a truly world-class ball-winning playmaker has yet to be introduced to the Parkhead fans.

SHUNSUKE NAKAMURA

Born: Yokohama, Japan, 24 June 1978
Celtic career: 2005 to 2007
Appearances and goals:

League		FA Cup		Lg Cup		Europe	
A	G	A	G	A	G	A	G
71/4	18	6	0	4	0	7/1	2

Total appearances: 88/5
Total goals: 20
League Championships: 2005-06; 2006-07
Scottish Cup: 2006-07
League Cup: 2005-06
Honours: 73 Japan caps

One of the biggest soccer stars in his native Japan, Shunsuke Nakamura has impressed the Celtic supporters with his flair, vision and ability since his move from Italian outfit Reggina for £2.5 million in the summer of 2005.

In 1997, 19-year-old Nakamura joined Yokohama Marinos of J League (later merged with Yokohama Flugels and renamed Yokohama F. Marinos) a club whose youth side he had played for when it was known as Nissan Motors FC. Within three years he had won the J League Most Valuable Player Award, and after a six-month loan period at Reggina, joined the Italian club on a permanent basis.

Having helped Japan win the Asian Cup 2000, he appeared to have cemented his place in the national team, but because manager Troussier believed he lacked the physique and stamina to cope, he was omitted from Japan's squad for the 2002 World Cup. After the tournament, Troussier

Shunsuke Nakamura off on a devastating run during Celtic's match against Shakhtar Donetsk in the 2007 Champions League (www.snspix.com)

resigned and new coach, the Brazilian Zico, immediately brought Nakamura back to the national team. He led Japan to the Championship at Asian Cup 2004 and played in all three games in the 2006 World Cup Finals, scoring the opening goal in the first game against Australia.

However, Nakamura struggled with injuries in the defensive-minded Serie A, and after three seasons in which Reggina struggled to avoid relegation, he decided it was time to move on. He expressed interest in playing in Spain, and reports linked him to Atletico Madrid and Deportivo La Coruna, as well as Bundesliga teams Borussia Dortmund and Borussia Monchengladbach, but Nakamura ultimately chose to join Celtic.

Though a number of observers warned that Nakamura's lack of pace and stamina might be a problem in Scotland, he made an immediate impact with Celtic as he was named Man of the Match on his debut against Dundee United. His creativity as well as his work ethic and composure under pressure won praise from team-mates, manager and supporters, and, in his first season with the club, in which he scored seven goals in 39 games, including two in a 4-1 defeat of Kilmarnock, he won his first major club titles, the Scottish Premier League and League Cup.

During the close season there was a lot of speculation linking Nakamura with a move to Spain or back to Reggina, but he signed a new contract, showing that he was fully behind the mission to retain the SPL title and advance in the Champion's League.

Having scored a superb free-kick to bring the Champions League game against Manchester United level at 2-2 (though United went on to win 3-2), Nakamura scored perhaps the most important goal of his career with a spectacular 30-yard free-kick against United at Parkhead in the return game. The goal resulted in the Hoops progressing to the Champions League knockout stage for the first time, and further secured his hero status with the Celtic fans.

Prior to this, in a League game against Dundee United at Tannadice, he netted the first hat-trick of his Celtic career in a 4-1 win—all his goals coming in the space of just 14 minutes. In the game against the same opposition at Parkhead on Boxing Day 2006, Nakamura earned Celtic a point with a stunning chip, and his performance in the latter stages of that game prompted manager Gordon Strachan to proclaim his creative superstar 'a genius'.

Having helped Celtic retain the League Championship and win the Scottish Cup by defeating Dunfermline, he was the recipient of three individual honours, being named both Scottish PFA and Football Writers' Player of the Year, as well as the SPL Player of the Season.

LEE NAYLOR

Born: Bloxwich, 19 March 1980
Celtic career: 2006 to 2007
Appearances and goals:

League		FA Cup		Lg Cup		Europe	
A	G	A	G	A	G	A	G
38	0	5	0	1	0	8	0

Total appearances: 52
Total goals: 0
League Championships: 2006-07

When the Hoops added Lee Naylor to their squad in the summer of 2006, they brought a player regarded by many as one of the most underrated players in England to a wider audience.

The Bloxwich-born player joined his local club Wolverhampton Wanderers and made his debut in the local derby against Birmingham City at St Andrew's in 1997. His displays for the Molineux club led to him winning Under-21 honours for England, and in 2000-01 he was voted the club's Player of the Year. He only really established himself in the Wolves side during 2002-03, when he was part of the squad that reached the play-off final at the Millennium Stadium.

He was the club's only ever-present in the Premiership campaign of 2003-04, and quite often was the youngest player on the pitch. Despite suffering from a number of niggling injuries, his surging runs and crosses became an important part of Wolves' attacking play under new manager Glenn Hoddle. He had spent nine seasons at Molineux and appeared in 334 games when, in August 2006, he signed for Celtic. His departure was a great blow to the Midlands club, for despite his experience, he was just 26 years old.

Though the Wolves boss Mick McCarthy was disappointed to see his left-back depart, he accepted the decision, saying 'When you've got a player who has done great for the club, if someone comes in for him and he gets the opportunity, I fully understand his desire to move on to fresh pastures.'

The lure of Champions League football was too much, and Naylor, who agreed a three-year contract with Gordon Strachan, soon became the Hoops' first-choice left-back. A good reader of the game and dangerous coming forward, particularly with his ability from dead-ball situations, Naylor went on to prove an important figure in Celtic's 2006-07 season.

He won a Player of the Month award for October 2006, and, over the first half of the season, convinced Celtic fans that he was an integral component of a Parkhead team competing in the last sixteen of the UEFA Champions League.

Having helped the Hoops win the SPL title and the Scottish Cup in his first season with the club, his performances for Celtic have exceeded all expectations. He even drew praise from England manager Steve McClaren, who revealed that the full-back was on a 'long-list' of players that he regularly monitored for the full England squad.

CHARLIE NICHOLAS

Born: Glasgow, 30 December 1961
Celtic career: 1979 to 1983 and 1990 to 1995
Appearances and goals:

League		FA Cup		Lg Cup		Europe	
A	**G**	**A**	**G**	**A**	**G**	**A**	**G**
159/28	85	9/2	7	24/7	26	16/4	7

Total appearances: 208/41
Total goals: 125
League Championships: 1980-81; 1981-82
League Cup: 1982-83
Honours: 20 Scotland caps

Idolised wherever he played, Charlie Nicholas burst onto the Scottish football scene in the 1980-81 season, netting 28 goals in 39 games for Celtic. A prolific goalscorer with superb technical ability who could prise open the meanest defence with one of his trademark flicks, Champagne Charlie joined his boyhood heroes from the Parkhead Boys' Club in the summer of 1979. A spell in the reserves was cut short when top clubs from south of the Border began to take an interest in the precocious teenager.

Elevated to the club's first team, he seized his chance, and six goals in ten appearances were already his, when during the 1981-82 season, he broke his leg playing for the reserves against Morton at Cappielow Park. However, he had played in enough games to help the Hoops retain the Championship.

He returned to the side with a bang in 1982-83, to head the scoring charts with an incredible 48 goals—not surprisingly he was Scotland's leading scorer—and was voted Scottish Footballer of the Year. Celtic full-back Danny McGrain later recalled how the young Nicholas became the centre of unwanted attention in a pub from a jealous lower league player, who said to him: 'I can do anything you can do, pal, anything!' To which Nicholas replied 'Oh yeah? Can you do this then?' He took out a £20 note and tore it up in front of the player's face. However, after the embarrassed player had stormed off, speechless, Charlie was seen recovering his money from the floor and borrowing sellotape!

His performances in that 1982-83 season tempted Arsenal boss Terry Neill to part with £650,000 to take him south to Highbury. He quickly became the toast of the North Bank, but he was not exactly the darling of the Gunners' new boss George Graham, and, despite scoring both goals in

Charlie Nicholas during the 1994-95 season (www.snspix.com)

Arsenal's 1987 League Cup win over Liverpool, he was on his way back north to Aberdeen in a £400,000 deal the following year.

However, a Scottish Cup Final victory over Celtic in 1990 was greeted with less than normal enthusiasm, so it was no surprise when he headed to Parkhead in the summer. He still possessed the ability to turn a game single-handedly, but, playing in one of the poorest Celtic sides for years, was unable to add to his collection of medals.

Nicholas, who gained 20 caps for Scotland between 1983 and 1989, signed for Clyde in 1995 before quitting the following season to take up a career in broadcasting. He now earns a living as a pundit on Sky Sports and as a part-time newspaper columnist. However, his forthright views on Scottish football, particularly about the national team during the ill-starred managerial tenure of Berti Vogts, earned him a number of enemies among both players and fans!

BRIAN O'NEIL

Born: Paisley, 6 September 1972
Celtic career: 1991 to 1997
Appearances and goals:

League		FA Cup		Lg Cup		Europe	
A	G	A	G	A	G	A	G
92/27	8	10	9	6/4	1	8/3	1

Total appearances: 116/34
Total goals: 19
Honours: 7 Scotland caps

Defensive midfielder Brian O'Neil started out with Celtic, but, despite showing talent in abundance, he tended to play off the pace of the game, and, in his early days at Parkhead, he was largely a fringe player.

After a loan spell in New Zealand with Porirua Viard, he rejoined the Hoops where his displays earned him selection for the Scotland Under-21 side. He had earlier represented Scotland in the World Youth Cup in 1989 and scored the goal against Portugal that put Young Scotland in the final. On the big day itself, he had a penalty saved by the Saudi keeper in normal time, and then missed another in the shoot-out!

Though he was a regular in the Celtic sides of the early 1990s, and played his part in helping the club reach the Scottish Cup Final of 1994-95, he was forced to miss the 1-0 win over Airdrie through injury, having impressed in the semi-final matches against Hibernian. Despite O'Neil winning the first of seven full caps for Scotland during the latter days of his time at Parkhead, domestic honours eluded him and he joined Nottingham Forest on loan.

Sadly for O'Neil this ended in injury, and he returned to Parkhead before signing for Aberdeen in an attempt to get his failing career back on track. After just one season at Pittodrie, he joined German club VfL Wolfsburg for £350,000, and enjoyed two fairly successful seasons on the continent before moving to England and Derby County in an exchange deal that saw Stefan Schnoor return to Germany.

Unfortunately, just two minutes into his Derby County debut against Manchester United, he suffered a serious knee injury that led to a long lay-off. Injuries again hampered his progress the following season, and in November 2002 his contract was terminated.

After a trial period with Preston North End, he secured a long-term contract, demonstrating a simple but effective passing game that improved the play of many of those around him, most notably Nigerian Dickson Etuhu. The following season he demonstrated his versatility by playing at centre-half during an injury crisis at the club.

Probably his best season at Deepdale was 2004-05, when his effort during games gave little indication that the years were taking their toll. Indeed, having helped the club reach the play-off final against West Ham United, he earned a surprise recall to the Scotland squad as fitting reward for his consistency.

The following season, O'Neil, who was worshipped by the Deepdale faithful, helped North End reach the play-offs again, but having played in the semi-final matches against Leeds United, he was forced to retire due to longstanding injury problems.

BERTIE PEACOCK

Born: Coleraine, Northern Ireland, 29 September 1928
Died: 22 July 2004
Celtic career: 1949 to 1961
Appearances and goals:

League		FA Cup		Lg Cup		Europe	
A	G	A	G	A	G	A	G
318	32	56	8	80	10	-	-

Total appearances: 454
Total goals: 50
League Championships: 1953-54
Scottish Cup: 1950-51; 1953-54
League Cup: 1956-57; 1957-58
Honours: 31 Northern Ireland caps

Having started his career with his home-town club Coleraine, Bertie Peacock joined Glentoran, for whom he scored the only goal of the 1949 Irish Cup Final against Barney Cannon's Derry City. Shortly afterwards he joined Celtic, and made his debut at inside-left in a Scottish League Cup tie against Aberdeen.

After netting the only goal of the game against East Fife on the opening day of the 1950-51 season, Bertie Peacock became an established member of the Celtic side. He was Charlie Tully's left-wing partner in the youngest-ever Hoops team to win the Scottish Cup, when Motherwell were beaten at Hampden Park in April 1951.

Northern Ireland picked him and Tully for the game against Scotland at Windsor Park in October 1951, but the visitors won! A year later, Peacock dropped back to left-half, and it wasn't long before the great Celtic half-back line of Evans, Stein and Peacock began to feature regularly for the Parkhead club.

After helping Celtic win the double in 1953-54, he was a member of the first-ever Celtic team to win the League Cup in 1956. He was then appointed Celtic's captain, and, in October 1957, led the club as they retained the trophy by hammering Rangers 7-1.

Peacock was part of the wonderful Irish performance in the World Cup of 1958, when his energy so impressed the Swedish journalists that they nicknamed him 'The Little Black Ant', because his jet-black hair seemed to be all over the park against Czechoslovakia (twice), Argentina and West Germany. In the play-off game against the Czechs, Peacock was badly injured, but still managed to 'score' a disallowed goal in extra time.

After missing the Scottish Cup Final against Hibs in 1961, he was fit for the replay, but was told he could play instead for Northern Ireland in Rome if he wanted. Celtic lost the Cup, while the discarded skipper played the three games of his life against Italy, Greece and West Germany, and all away from home.

Peacock, who scored 50 goals in 454 games, was an all-time Celtic great and not a bad manager either, taking charge of the Northern Ireland international team from 1962 to 1967, and later taking his beloved Coleraine to their first-ever Irish League Championship in 1973-74. In 1986 he was awarded the MBE for his services to football.

Bertie Peacock was a legend. During his playing days, he was worshipped, as a manager he was respected, but it was as a person, it came as a package. At home in Coleraine, until his death in 2004, he was a God, and in Glasgow, he will always be remembered as one of their very best! In the summer of 2006 a statue of Bertie Peacock was commissioned. The memorial is to stand in Coleraine and was unveiled in July 2007 at the opening of the 25th Milk Cup, of which he was one of the founders.

STEPHEN PEARSON

Born: Lanark, 2 October 1982
Celtic career: 2004 to 2007
Appearances and goals:

League		FA Cup		Lg Cup		Europe	
A	G	A	G	A	G	A	G
22/34	6	5/1	0	3/1	0	6/4	1

Total appearances: 36/40
Total goals: 7
League Championships: 2003-04; 2005-06
Scottish Cup: 2003-04
Honours: 6 Scotland caps

A lifelong Celtic fan, Stephen Pearson joined his boyhood heroes in a £350,000 deal from Motherwell in January 2004, being widely regarded as one of the most talented young midfielders in Scotland.

As a boy, Pearson attended the renowned Our Lady's High School in Motherwell—the school's famous footballing alumni including the likes of Sir Matt Busby, Billy McNeill and Bobby Murdoch. Like most of his fellow pupils, he grew up a Hoops fan, but it was to be at Motherwell that he would start his career.

Motherwell were a financially troubled club at this time, and, in 2002, they were placed in administration to prevent liquidation, with 19 senior players released. This did mean, however, that talented young players like Pearson and the fast-emerging James McFadden gained instant elevation to first team status, and a chance to develop their skills more quickly than contemporaries at other clubs. The rewards of this policy soon became clear, and, with the Steelmen in a comfortable mid-table position, Pearson received his first Scotland cap in a memorable 1-0 victory over Holland.

However, the club's financial predicament ensured they were unable to refuse any reasonable offers for a player, and when Martin O'Neill offered £350,000, Pearson fulfilled a childhood ambition by moving to Parkhead. An injury to John Hartson enabled him to hold down a regular place in the team for the rest of that campaign. His fine form continued, notably in Celtic's epic UEFA Cup defeat of Barcelona, and he won the Scottish PFA Young Player of the Year for the 2003-04 season, when he helped the Hoops win the Scottish League and Cup double.

Unable to match his achievements of the previous season in 2004-05, and despite continuing to appear for the national team, his first team opportunities at Parkhead were limited due to injury. He was hampered by injuries again the following season, making just three starts, but he did make 17 appearances from the bench and scored a crucial goal against Hearts at Tynecastle as Celtic came from behind to win 3-2.

In the 2006 close season, Pearson was strongly linked with a move away from Parkhead, with former Motherwell manager Billy Davies, now in charge of Derby County, expressing an interest. But the departure of Stiliyan Petrov to Aston Villa gave Pearson an opportunity to regain his place in the Celtic midfield. He went on to score Celtic's third goal against Benfica in the club's Champions League home game, describing the goal as 'the moment of my career'.

In January 2007, Pearson did part company with Celtic, signing for Derby County for a fee believed to be just under £1 million. He was instrumental in the Rams reaching the play-off final, where it was his goal that defeated West Bromwich Albion and earned the Pride Park club a place in the Premiership.

STILIYAN PETROV

Born: Montana, Bulgaria, 5 July 1979
Celtic career: 1999 to 2006
Appearances and goals:

League		FA Cup		Lg Cup		Europe	
A	G	A	G	A	G	A	G
215/13	55	15/3	5	9/5	0	49/2	4

Total appearances: 288/23
Total goals: 64
League Championships: 2000-01; 2001-02; 2003-04; 2005-06
Scottish Cup: 2003-04; 2004-05
League Cup: 2005-06
Honours: 68 Bulgaria caps

One of Celtic's most popular players of recent years, Petrov wrote his autobiography with the assistance of Sunday Mail sports journalist Mark Guidi, and entitled it *You Can Call Me Stan*, in reference to his nickname 'Stan', a shortened form of his given name.

He began his career with his Bulgerian home-town side FC Montana. His form soon attracted the bigger clubs, and, a year after making his professional debut, he moved on to CSKA Sofia where it didn't take him long to break into their first team. He emerged as one of Bulgaria's bright young talents, and he was soon playing for the national side. Having made his international debut in 1999, he went on to captain the national side and win a total of 68 caps, before surprisingly announcing his retirement from international football in October 2006.

Petrov joined Celtic in a £2 million deal in the summer of 1999, and despite struggling a little in his first season in Scottish football, it wasn't long before things started going his way.

He was voted SPL Young Player of the Year in 2001, in spite of a serious leg break. He played an important part and scored some crucial goals as the Hoops enjoyed Champions League and UEFA Cup runs and secured domestic title success.

The 2003-04 campaign was a good one for Petrov. He scored 10 goals in 55 games, including the third and winning goal in the Scottish Cup Final win over Dunfermline Athletic, and led Bulgaria to Euro 2004. He played in all three of their group games—being sent off against Denmark—before they were eliminated from the tournament.

The following season saw his fine form continue. He put in a series of impressive performances for both club and country, as Celtic narrowly missed out on the SPL title but claimed the Scottish Cup. The only downer in his season came in the final league match against Rangers in which he scored the opener, but was then hit by a plastic cup thrown by a fan!

He continued to shine in 2005-06, playing 45 games and adding a further 10 goals. A personal highlight for Petrov was a hat-trick in the 5-0 defeat of Motherwell. At the end of the season, Petrov, who had scored 64 goals in 311 games from midfield, asked for a transfer, this in spite of signing a contract the previous January. Despite a reported £5 million interest from Portsmouth, he ended up signing for former boss Martin O'Neill at Aston Villa for £6.5 million.

Inspirational on his debut against West Ham United, Petrov only showed flashes of the form that had made him such a big hit at Parkhead. A creative and tenacious player and hugely popular in the dressing-room, he will be hoping to improve on things in future games.

DAVIE PROVAN

Born: Gourock, 8 May 1956
Celtic career: 1978 to 1986
Appearances and goals:

League		FA Cup		Lg Cup		Europe	
A	G	A	G	A	G	A	G
192/14	28	29	2	41/1	11	25/1	1

Total appearances: 287/16
Total goals: 42
League Championships: 1978-79; 1980-81; 1981-82; 1985-86
Scottish Cup: 1979-80; 1984-85
League Cup: 1982-83
Honours: 10 Scotland caps

It was a moment of pure genius towards the end of the 1984-85 Scottish Cup Final that earned Davie Provan his rightful place in Celtic folklore. 'Only two goals have ever been scored direct from free-kicks in the Scottish Cup Final. Is this history in the making?' were the prophetic utterings of commentator Archie MacPherson who, a few seconds later, was describing Dundee United keeper Hamish McAlpine picking Provan's exquisitely struck 20-yard curler out of the back of the net. Frank McGarvey scored a last-gasp winner to ensure the trophy returned to Parkhead, but, quite rightly, the match will always be remembered for that Davie Provan goal.

Davie Provan (left) and Frank McGarvey celebrate victory over Dundee United in the 1985 Scottish Cup Final (www.snspix.com)

A former shipping clerk, Davie Provan began his first-class career with Kilmarnock in 1974 after a brief spell with junior club Port Glasgow Rovers. An old-fashioned winger in the mould of the great Jimmy Johnstone, he possessed a lethal shot in either foot and the ability to deliver the most accurate of crosses. Billy McNeill, who had tried to sign him while he was at Pittodrie, paid his former Celtic team-mate Willie Fernie £120,000 to bring Provan to Parkhead in September 1978.

The move paid instant dividends, and Provan helped deliver the League Championship title later that year, when choosing the infamous 4-2 Championship decider against arch-rivals Rangers at Parkhead to produce his best-ever game in the green and white.

Two further Championships, a Scottish Cup and a Scottish League Cup followed in the next three years, during which time Provan picked up 10 full caps for Scotland and was nominated Scottish Player of the Year in 1980.

The viral complaint that led to Davie Provan's retirement first manifested itself during the 3-0 defeat against Rangers at Ibrox in November 1985. As the second half got under way, he felt totally listless and drained. It was over a year later before he was diagnosed as having Myalgic Encephalomyelitis (ME).

Celtic fans were given one last chance to witness his skill, and a crowd of 40,000 turned up for his swansong in a testimonial match against Nottingham Forest in December 1987.

He remained on the groundstaff at Parkhead, helping Jinky Johnstone with coaching the club's youngsters. These days, he is recognised as one of the finest TV and radio broadcasters on the game north of the Border.

RONNIE SIMPSON

Born: Glasgow, 11 October 1930
Died: 20 April 2004
Celtic career: 1964 to 1970
Appearances and goals:

League		FA Cup		Lg Cup		Europe	
A	G	A	G	A	G	A	G
118	0	17	0	29	0	23	0

Total appearances: 187

Total goals: 0

League Championships: 1965-66; 1966-67; 1967-68; 1968-69
Scottish Cup: 1966-67
League Cup: 1965-66; 1967-68
European Cup: 1966-67
Honours: 5 Scotland caps

Over nine years had elapsed since goalkeeper Ronnie Simpson last tasted glory, and a £4,000 transfer from Hibernian to Celtic in September 1964 was generally regarded as one last pay-day before the boots were hung up. But the superbly agile shot-stopper was to cram in more awards over the next five years with the Hoops than he could have dared imagine when making his debut for Queen's Park, aged just 14 years and 234 days!

After a distinguished amateur career which saw him play for Great Britain, including two appearances in the 1948 Olympic Games, Simpson had signed professional forms for Third Lanark. Following National Service, he moved to Newcastle United in 1951, and here he enjoyed a nine-year stay in the English First Division, a stint highlighted by two FA Cup winners' medals, against Arsenal in 1951-52 and Manchester City three seasons later, before returning north of the Border to join Hibs in October 1960.

Ronnie Simpson's positional sense was immaculate, and, despite his relative lack of inches for a keeper, he had little trouble cutting out the most accurate crosses from either wing.

After four years at Easter Road, and at a time when most players are contemplating retirement, he joined Celtic. He was sold to the Parkhead club by then Hibs boss Jock Stein, but ironically it was the 'Big Man' who reignited his career at Parkhead after the two had buried their differences.

Known as 'Faither' to his younger team-mates, Ronnie Simpson played 187 times for Celtic, following his debut against Barcelona in an Inter Cities Fairs Cup tie in November 1964, keeping a remarkable 90 clean sheets— almost one every two games—while amassing four League Championships, a Scottish Cup and two League Cup winners' medals.

Capped for the first time in April 1967 in a European Championship victory over World Champions England, a further four were to follow, and Simpson was named Scottish Player of the Year a month later, before crowning his glittering career with a European Cup winners' medal with the famous Lisbon Lions.

A shoulder injury forced Simpson to quit the game in 1970, and he missed out on one last bow when, with the League title already won for the sixth successive year, Jock Stein decided to parade the Lions of Lisbon one last time against Clyde in May 1971.

After a spell coaching for the Parkhead club, he managed Hamilton Academical before leaving the game to embark on a life which took in many occupations. A fine golfer and a past winner of the 'Footballers Championship', Ronnie Simpson was one of those rare footballers who enjoyed two long and successful careers either side of the Border.

ERIC SMITH

Born: Glasgow, 29 July 1934
Died: Dubai, 12 June 1991
Celtic career: 1953 to 1960
Appearances and goals:

League		FA Cup		Lg Cup		Europe	
A	**G**	**A**	**G**	**A**	**G**	**A**	**G**
95	12	19	5	16	3	-	-

Total appearances: 130
Total goals: 20
Honours: 2 Scotland caps

Though he had made his Celtic debut against Queen of the South in a 1-1 home draw in October 1954, and been on the tour of Ireland the following summer, Smith couldn't win a regular place in the Parkhead club's side. That is, until August 1955, when he was given the inside-left berth against Rangers in a League Cup tie. Smith scored twice in the space of five minutes in the first half, as the Hoops went on to win 4-1 at Ibrox.

A year later, in the Glasgow Cup, he led a famous fightback in an Old Firm game. With Rangers 3-0 up at half-time, Smith scored immediately after the interval before inspiring his side to victory.

Over the next few seasons, Smith, who had been in the Celtic side that lost the 1956 Scottish Cup Final to Hearts 3-1, saw his versatility exploited by the Hoops who played him at half-back, on both wings and at inside-forward.

Even so, it was 1957-58 before he really established himself in the Celtic side, where his no-nonsense, all-action approach made him hugely popular among Celtic supporters. His form for Celtic led to him winning two caps for the national side in 1959 in matches against Holland and Portugal, when he played at inside-right.

By 1960 he was back in his favoured position of right-half, but by now had become the club's third-choice in that position, though he did play on the right-wing in the Scottish Cup game at Elgin City in March 1960, when his goal in the 89th minute saved the Hoops from a rather ignominious draw!

In the summer of 1960 he joined Don Revie's Leeds United for a fee of £10,000, where it was anticipated that his experience and grit would stiffen the Yorkshire club's defence, but that idea was scuppered when he broke a leg in his first season at the club. In June 1966 he went to Morton, retiring two years later and working for a spell as coach with the Greenock club. He became the manager for a short time in 1972 after spending some time in Cyprus as coach to Pezoporikos Larnaca.

Shortly after recommending one of his young Morton players—Joe

Jordan—to Leeds, he was appointed manager of Hamilton Academical, and he held that job for six years until taking over the reins of Sharjah FC in the United Arab Emirates. Between June 1982 and May 1983 he was assistant-manager to Don Revie at Al Nasr, becoming manager of Al Shaab the following year. He then returned to Cyprus to coach Pezopokoris for a second time, and was still in post when he died of a heart attack on holiday in Dubai.

JOCK STEIN

Born: Earnock, 6 October 1922
Died: Cardiff, 10 September 1985
Celtic career: 1951 to 1957
Appearances and goals:

League		FA Cup		Lg Cup		Europe	
A	G	A	G	A	G	A	G
106	2	21	0	20	0	-	-

Total appearances: 147
Total goals: 2
League Championships: 1953-54
Scottish Cup: 1953-54

Known throughout the footballing world as the 'Big Man'—a tag he neither sought nor really felt at ease with—Jock Stein single-handedly changed the fortunes of Celtic Football Club, turning them from the proverbial under-achieving sleeping giants into Champions of Europe. Within a couple of months of arriving at Parkhead, Stein ended the Hoops' seven-year trophy famine by guiding them to Scottish Cup glory over Dunfermline Athletic, the club where he cut his teeth in management after a spell in charge of Celtic's second string.

By his own admission, Jock Stein could never be regarded as a 'top drawer' player. A tall, gangling figure, he started out with Blantyre Victoria before, still working as a miner, he joined Albion Rovers in 1942. Following a wages dispute, he joined non-League Llanelli, and his return to Scotland as a Celtic player in December 1951 was a surprise. Stein made his debut against St Mirren, and, after winning a regular spot, was appointed the club's captain.

He helped Celtic win the Coronation Cup in 1953, and had it not been for his organisational skills, the club would probably have not won the League and Cup double the following year. A natural leader, his playing career was cut short by an ankle injury sustained in a League Cup tie against Rangers in 1955. An attempted rehabilitation failed, and Stein wore the green and white hoops for the last time in a friendly against Coleraine in 1956.

After what chairman Bob Kelly described as 'farming out' period at East

End Park and later Hibernian, Stein returned to Parkhead in March 1965 to take over the reins of the great club, as only the third manager in their 77-year history. In one of his early team meetings, Stein told his squad, 'Celtic jerseys are not for second best. They don't shrink to fit inferior players.'

A period of unprecedented success followed as the Big Man moulded a bunch of talented individuals into one of the most feared attacking teams in Europe, which delivered nine successive League titles, six Scottish Cups, six League Cups and the European Cup in 1967, to equal the world record. Following Celtic's win over Inter Milan, Liverpool boss Bill Shankly congratulated him: 'John, you're immortal now'.

Stein almost lost his life in a horrific car crash in 1975, but recovered to lead the Hoops to the League and Cup double of 1976-77 before making way for Billy McNeill a year later. An ill-fated 44-day stint as manager of Leeds United followed, before he returned home to take charge of the national side.

He led Scotland to their third successive World Cup Finals in Spain in 1982 and had guided them to within touching distance of Mexico '86 when a fatal heart attack claimed his life at a vital qualifier in Cardiff in September 1985. Stein commanded the respect of players and managers alike, but was never afraid to put a so-called star in his place, while finding time to listen to the youngest member of his groundstaff.

CHRIS SUTTON

Born: Nottingham, 10 March 1973
Celtic career: 2000 to 2006
Appearances and goals:

League		FA Cup		Lg Cup		Europe	
A	G	A	G	A	G	A	G
127/3	63	16	5	8/1	2	42/2	16

Total appearances: 193/6
Total goals: 86
League Championships: 2000-01; 2001-02; 2003-04
Scottish Cup: 2000-01; 2003-04; 2004-05
League Cup: 2000-01
Honours: 1 England cap

Chris Sutton, who holds the record for the quickest goal ever in an Old Firm clash, scoring after just 18 seconds of the game at Ibrox in 2002, was Martin O'Neill's first signing when Celtic forked out £6 million for his services in the summer of 2000.

Able to play either in defence, midfield or attack, Chris Sutton started out with Norwich City, and, in 1991-92, he was part of the Canaries side that spent most of the new Premiership campaign as leaders before eventually

Chris Sutton competes for a high ball with David McCracken of Dundee United in a 2004 SPL clash (www.snspix.com)

slipping back to third place. In July 1994, Sutton became the most expensive player in English football when he was transferred to Blackburn Rovers for £5 million.

In his first season at Ewood Park, he developed a strong partnership up front with Alan Shearer and scored 15 Premiership goals to secure the club's first league title since 1913-14. A succession of injuries combined with a loss of form saw him make just three starts in 1995-96, but he regained his old form over the next three seasons and even won an England cap in November 1997, although he was left out of England's World Cup squad after a fall-out with national coach Glenn Hoddle.

At the end of the 1998-99 season, Rovers were relegated and Sutton was sold to Chelsea for £10 million. His time at Stamford Bridge proved an unhappy one, as he struggled to live up to the price tag and adapt to

Chelsea's style of play. He even failed to make the bench for the club's FA Cup Final win over Aston Villa and was sold to Celtic.

He scored the winner on his Hoops' debut against Dundee United, and in his first Old Firm match against Rangers, he scored the first and last goals in a dramatic 6-2 victory for Celtic in a match that was tagged 'The Demolition Derby'. It was even more unusual in that in a press conference before the game, Sutton was asked why he was here in Scotland. He replied 'To put Rangers in their place.'

Sutton formed a prolific partnership with Swedish international Henrik Larsson, one to rival his earlier one with Shearer. His long ball to set up Larsson's equaliser in the 2004 Scottish Cup Final was a perfect example of the link-up play between the two. These qualities were recognised by his fellow professionals and he was voted SPFA Player of the Year for season 2003-04. His goals helped Celtic win three League Championships, three Scottish Cups and a League Cup during his time at Parkhead. They also, of course, reached the UEFA Cup Final, where they went down to Porto.

On leaving Celtic, Sutton joined Birmingham City on a free transfer in January 2006, but injuries restricted his appearances and his only goal came in the derby defeat to Aston Villa. Following Birmingham's relegation, Sutton signed for Aston Villa until the end of the 2006-07 season—the move seeing him link up with former Celtic boss Martin O'Neill. However, an eye injury sustained in a game against Manchester United forced his retirement from the game.

ALAN THOMPSON

Born: Newcastle, 22 December 1973
Celtic career: 2000 to 2007
Appearances and goals:

League		FA Cup		Lg Cup		Europe	
A	**G**	**A**	**G**	**A**	**G**	**A**	**G**
146/12	37	19/1	4	8/3	2	34/4	8

Total appearances: 197/20
Total goals: 51
League Championships: 2000-01; 2001-02; 2003-04; 2005-06
Scottish Cup: 2000-01; 2003-04; 2004-05
Honours: 1 England cap

Alan Thompson's career has been plagued with injury. In 1989 he was involved in a near-fatal car crash, breaking his neck in five places. He defied medical expectation and managed to return to professional football.

He started off as a trainee with his home-town club Newcastle United, before moving to Bolton Wanderers in 1993, where he became an integral part of the Trotters' team which won promotion to the Premier League on two occasions—in 1994-95 and 1996-97. Thompson also scored Bolton's goal in the 1995 League Cup Final as they lost 2-1 to Liverpool. While with Bolton, Thompson had won England Under-21 honours, but when the Lancashire club were relegated in 1997-98, he joined Aston Villa for £4.5 million.

The midfielder added width on the left when playing in a 4-4-2 formation, or accurate passing and great vision from the centre of midfield when in a 3-5-2 formation. Injuries limited the number of appearances he was able to make during a two-year spell at Villa Park, and, in September 2000, Thompson decided to try his luck in Scotland and moved to Celtic for a fee of £2.75 million in what was Martin O'Neill's first season.

His move to the Hoops has brought the best out of Alan Thompson. The hardworking and tenacious midfielder helped the club win the League and Scottish Cup in his first season, but he enjoyed his best season in 2003-04 when the club not only repeated that achievement, but Thompson scored 11 league goals in 26 games. His form led to him winning full international honours in March of that season when he played for Sven Goran Eriksson's team against Sweden. After such an outstanding year, he signed a deal tying him to the Parkhead club until 2007.

Thompson continued his fine form into the 2004-05 campaign, playing 44 times and scoring 10 goals, including the only goal of the Scottish Cup Final as Dundee United were beaten 1-0. Thompson also scored the winning goal against Rangers in two separate Old Firm derby matches, but did have mixed fortunes in these encounters, being sent off twice!

The 2005-06 season saw him in competition for a midfield berth with Roy Keane and a fit-again Shaun Maloney, yet he still made enough appearances to pick up his fourth League Championship winners' medal. After a somewhat difficult pre-season, Thompson criticised the club's pre-season commitments and was sent home from their American training camp for an apparently non-existent thigh injury. Out of favour, there were times when Thompson didn't even secure a place on the substitute's bench, and, in January 2007, he secured a loan move to Leeds United until the end of the season.

Despite scoring on his debut against high-flying West Bromwich Albion and netting from a trademark free-kick against fellow-strugglers Hull City, he was unable to prevent the Elland Road club from losing their Championship status. He was made club captain for the 2007-8 season, hoping to lead the Yorkshire side back into the Championship, despite the 15-point penalty the club incurred after going into administration.

CHARLIE TULLY

Born: Belfast, 11 July 1924
Died: Belfast, 27 July 1971
Celtic career: 1948 to 1959
Appearances and goals:

League		FA Cup		Lg Cup		Europe	
A	**G**	**A**	**G**	**A**	**G**	**A**	**G**
215	30	34	7	69	8	-	-

Total appearances: 318
Total goals: 45
League Championships: 1953-54
Scottish Cup: 1950-51; 1953-54
League Cup: 1956-57; 1957-58
Honours: 10 Northern Ireland caps

Following the threat of relegation in 1947-48, Celtic moved quickly to sign Charlie Tully from Belfast Celtic for a fee of £8,000. A year earlier he had come to the club's attention when playing in a five-a-side competition in the RUC Sports in Belfast.

Though he made a quiet debut against Morton on the opening day of the 1948-49 league season, a few weeks later he became the idol of the Celtic fans after a remarkable display in the Old Firm game against Rangers' famed Iron Curtain defence, in a 3-1 win at Parkhead. Tully's audacious dribbling and astute passing skills ripped the Light Blues to shreds, and, for the older fans in the 70,000 crowd, evoked memories of the incomparable Patsy Gallacher.

It wasn't long before 'Tully mania' set in—'Tully' cocktails in the pubs, 'Tully' ties in the outfitters and a special green-flavoured 'Tully' ice cream. Tully, who possessed great skill on the field of play, also possessed a ready wit off it and was a newspaperman's dream. However, with the publicity came controversy, and the infamous Cox-Tully incident at Ibrox in 1949. Tully, who had appeared to have lost the ball in the Rangers box, was kicked in the stomach by full-back Sammy Cox, but the referee failed to award a penalty and waved play on. This resulted in 'bottle parties' and fights on the terraces. The upshot of this was that the SFA reprimanded both players and the clubs, but it was hard to see what Tully had done wrong!

Within the space of a few weeks in the summer of 1950, Charlie Tully had shared a joke with American actor/comedian Danny Kaye, sung along with Bing Crosby on a cruise and been welcomed as a member of the Celtic squad by the Pope. Back in Glasgow, they were saying that people in the Vatican that day were asking just who was that man with Charlie Tully!

However, Tully will be remembered for other key incidents and matches: inspiring the Hoops to a fightback when two goals down to Aberdeen in the 1951 St Mungo Cup, by winning a controversial corner after playing a throw-in off a defender's back; scoring against Falkirk at Brockville in the 1953 Scottish Cup from a corner kick, not once but twice—since the referee ordered the kick to be retaken; reducing Rangers to panic as outside-right in the famous 7-1 victory in the 1957 Cup Final.

He played 10 times for Northern Ireland, and, in 1952, scored both his country's goals in a 2-2 draw with England—and one came direct from a corner-kick!

On retiring as a player, he subsequently managed Irish outfits Cork, Hibs and Bangor. Charlie Tully died in his sleep in July 1971, and John Rafferty of *The Observer* wrote 'It was strange he should have gone out so peacefully. It was not his way of life.' Huge crowds attended his funeral in Belfast, and Celtic players and officials travelled across the Irish Sea to pay their last respects to one of Parkhead's greatest players.

STANISLAV VARGA

Born: Lipany, Slovakia, 8 October 1972
Celtic career: 2003 to 2006
Appearances and goals:

League		FA Cup		Lg Cup		Europe	
A	G	A	G	A	G	A	G
79/1	10	10	2	3/1	1	22	1

Total appearances: 114/2
Total goals: 14
League Championships: 2003-04; 2005-06
Scottish Cup: 2003-04; 2004-05
Honours: 56 Slovakia caps

A tall and commanding centre-back, Stanislav Varga started out with Tatran Presov before his consistent displays at the heart of the club's defence persuaded Slovan Bratislava to secure his services in 1998.

He was recruited for Sunderland for a fee of £650,000 by their then boss Peter Reid during the summer of 2000, and he began his career at the Stadium of Light with an impressive opening day display in Sunderland's 1-0 victory over Arsenal, comfortably picking up the Man of the Match award. Varga was first spotted by Peter Reid when playing for Slovakia in a friendly game against Norway before Euro 2000, and impressed the Black Cats' boss with the way he kept Tore Andrew Flo and Ole Gunnar Solskjaer out of the game.

Though he was a relative unknown in England, Varga, who has won over 50 international caps for Slovakia, enjoys nothing short of hero status in his home country, where thousands of fans watched his every step in the Premiership and then in the Scottish Premier League when he moved to Celtic.

Injuries began to hamper his progress at Sunderland, and he spent the latter part of the 2001-02 season on loan at West Bromwich Albion. On his return to the north-east he never really found his way back into the team, and in January 2003 he was released.

Less than a month later, Celtic boss Martin O'Neill snapped up the defender on a short-term deal. Despite only making one appearance for the Hoops in that time, he was rewarded with a two-year contract in July 2003. He missed just one game in 2003-04, helping his new team-mates to domestic glory with League Championship and Scottish Cup success.

The success continued in the 2004-05 season as he proved to be a rock at the heart of the Celtic defence. He even got up the park to score six times, including the goal in the Hoops' unlucky 3-1 defeat to the mighty AC Milan in the UEFA Champions League Group Stage. He played an important part in the run-in as the club won the 2005-06 League title, but as the following season got under way, he returned to Sunderland under new manager Roy Keane, a former Celtic colleague, along with Celtic's Ross Wallace, for a combined fee of £1.1 million.

His strong and powerful presence, ability in the air and no-nonsense defending made him a great favourite in his second spell at the Stadium of Light. Though there were occasions when he found himself warming the bench, there is no doubt that Varga played his part in the Wearsiders' winning automatic promotion to the Premiership.

JAN VENNEGOOR OF HESSELINK

Born: Oldenzaal, Holland, 7 November 1978
Celtic career: 2006 to 2007
Appearances and goals:

League		FA Cup		Lg Cup		Europe	
A	G	A	G	A	G	A	G
23/4	18	4	4	1	0	4	1

Total appearances: 32/4
Total goals: 23
League Championships: 2006-07
Scottish Cup: 2006-07
Honours: 13 Holland caps

A prolific goalscorer in his native Holland with FC Twente and PSV Eindhoven, the man with the most unusual name in European football, who was also a target for Porto and Bolton Wanderers, was brought to Celtic by Gordon Strachan in a £3.4 million deal in August 2006.

His name—the longest in European football—derives from the 17th century, when two farming families in the Enschede area of Holland intermarried. Both the Vennegoor and Hesselink names carried equal social

Jan Vennegoor of Hesselink takes the ball past AC Milan's Andrea Pirlo (left) and Rino Gattuso in a 2007 Champions League tie at Celtic Park which ended all square (www.snspix.com)

weight and so—rather than choose between them—they chose to use both. 'Of' in Dutch translates to 'or' in English, which means that a translation of his name would read Jan Vennegoor or Hesselink!

Jan Vennegoor of Hesselink scored 59 league goals for FC Twente over the course of five seasons, before joining PSV Eindhoven in the summer of 2001. He quickly became accustomed to finding the net there too, scoring 22 goals in his first season. However, the second and third seasons at PSV proved less fruitful, and though he was told he could leave, he decided to stay on.

He was outstanding in 2004-05 and, having won his first international cap against Portugal in October 2000, he earned a recall to the national side after an absence of four-and-a-half years. He scored 19 goals in 28 matches, and continued in similar vein the following season. He had scored 72 goals in 156 league outings when he signed a three-year deal with Celtic, with the option of a further year.

He scored on his debut after coming off the bench against Hibernian, and in his next game against Aberdeen, he scored the winner from outside the box in a 1-0 win. He then scored his first European goal for the Hoops in the Champions League encounter with Manchester United.

Injuries subsequently curtailed his first team appearances, but towards the end of the campaign he came into some form, netting his first hat-trick for the Parkhead club against St Mirren and a last minute winner against Inverness Caledonian Thistle. He then received his marching orders, after receiving a second booking for leaving the field of play to celebrate with the Celtic fans!

A towering presence in the penalty box and comfortable with the ball at his feet, he also scored the opening goal against Kilmarnock, the game in which the Hoops retained the League Championship for the first time in five years—Shunsuke Nakamura scored a last-minute winner after Gary Wales had equalised for Killie. He rounded off a memorable first season with the club with a Scottish Cup winners' medal following Celtic's 1-0 defeat of Dunfermline Athletic.

MARK VIDUKA

Born: Melbourne, Australia, 9 October 1975
Celtic career: 1998 to 2004
Appearances and goals:

League		FA Cup		Lg Cup		Europe	
A	G	A	G	A	G	A	G
36/1	30	3	3	4	1	4	1

Total appearances: 47/1
Total goals: 35
League Cup: 1999-2000
Honours: 43 Australia caps

Regarded as a skilled player, able to hold the ball up well and bring other players into the game, Mark Viduka was voted Scottish Premier League Player of the Year after scoring 27 goals in his first full season with the Hoops.

Viduka started his career—where he is affectionately known as 'Big Dukes'—with Melbourne Knights in 1993, and became an Australian international in the summer of the following year. In his two seasons with Melbourne Knights he was top goalscorer in the National Soccer League, and was twice awarded the Johnny Warren Medal for NSL Player of the Year. His time with the Melbourne Knights also included winning the NSL title in 1994-95.

After that success, he moved to Croatia to play for Dinamo Zagreb, where he stayed for three years and made appearances in the UEFA Cup. In December 1998 Celtic splashed out £3.5 million for his services, though he had to wait a couple of months before making his debut off the bench in a 2-1 defeat of Dundee United. On his first start the following week, the

Australian gave a foretaste of what was to come by netting twice in a 5-1 win at Aberdeen. He scored another brace in a 4-2 win at Hearts and ended the campaign with five goals in eight starts.

He started the following season with two goals on the opening day, as Celtic put another five goals past Aberdeen at Pittodrie, later netting his first hat-trick for the club in a 5-1 mauling of Kilmarnock. Midway through the season he scored in 10 consecutive league games, including Celtic's goal in the 1-1 home draw with Rangers. Though injuries kept him out of action for the last few weeks of that 1999-2000 season, he had already won his first domestic honour with the Hoops after they had beaten Aberdeen 2-0 to lift the League Cup.

However, Viduka's occasionally lackadaisical attitude infuriated a section of the Celtic faithful, and a widely-reported quote where he announced that he was 'playing to only about 70% of my capacity up here in Scotland' did not endear him to either the fans or his fellow team-mates!

Leeds United manager David O'Leary signed Viduka just before the start of the 2000-01 season for a fee of £6 million. Forming a partnership with Alan Smith in the club's UEFA Champions League matches and Robbie Keane in the Premiership, Viduka scored 22 goals in his first season, including all four in a 4-3 defeat of Liverpool. In the 2002-03 season he scored another 22 goals, but the club's off-pitch financial troubles prompted the club to sell key players. Viduka stayed another season but the Elland Road club's relegation saw him sold to Middlesbrough.

His first season at the Riverside saw him frustrated by injuries; however, in 2005-06, he was in sensational form in all competitions. He played an important part in spearheading Boro's campaign in the UEFA Cup, where they reached the final only to lose to Sevilla. Newly-appointed Middlesbrough manager Gareth Southgate expressed his interest in keeping the Australian international, but in the summer of 2007 he became Newcastle United manager Sam Allardyce's first signing, scoring his first goal against his former club.

ANDY WALKER

Born: Glasgow, 6 April 1965
Celtic career: 1987 to 1992 and 1994 to 1996
Appearances and goals:

League		FA Cup		Lg Cup		Europe	
A	**G**	**A**	**G**	**A**	**G**	**A**	**G**
112/38	49	11/5	6	15/7	10	7/3	4

Total appearances: 148/53
Total goals: 69
League Championships: 1987-88

A striker of lightning-quick reflexes, Andy Walker began his career with Baillieston Juniors before joining Motherwell. Having made his debut at Meadowbank Thistle in December 1984, he scored the goal against Brechin City which clinched promotion the following May. They would have suffered relegation twelve months later but for League re-organisation, although Walker himself did manage to score against both Celtic and Rangers. He was the Steelmen's leading scorer in 1986-87, but kicked off the following season with Celtic after a £350,000 move.

His first season at Parkhead was hugely successful, as the Hoops won the double in their centenary season and Walker, who scored 31 goals in all competitions, won the first of three full international caps for Scotland in the match against Colombia. He showed, over the course of that season, that he possessed a thunderous shot and was a superb header of the ball, but in the League crunch match against Rangers at Ibrox in March 1988, he chested the ball over the line! Also it was his two late goals against Dundee the following month that clinched the Championship for Celtic. Walker's last minute goal in the Scottish Cup semi-final against Hearts sent the Hoops' fans into delirium as they then went on to win the trophy, beating Dundee United 2-1 in the final.

The following few seasons were less fruitful however, though he was forced to miss the 1989 Scottish Cup Final because of a horrendous injury at Aberdeen when Brian Irvine smacked the ball into his face and almost detached a retina. As the Hoops began to struggle at League level, Walker had his first taste of the English game when he played a couple of games on loan for Newcastle United.

In January 1992 he joined Bolton Wanderers on loan before the deal was made permanent. At Burnden Park he established a prolific partnership with John McGinlay as the Lancashire side earned promotion to the First Division in 1992-93. That same season he famously scored at Anfield to help the Trotters knock holders Liverpool out of the FA Cup. His season's total of 33 goals equalled a post-war club record set by Nat Lofthouse twice in the 1950s. He continued his scoring feats the following season until sustaining a serious knee injury against Swansea City.

Upon recovery he was the subject of a surprise bid from Celtic, who paid £550,000 to take him back to Parkhead.

The 1994-95 season was a mixed one for Walker. He won a Scotland recall, but the Hoops struggled in the League and suffered a shock defeat by Raith Rovers in the League Cup Final. Due to the arrival of Andreas Thom, Walker was again deemed surplus to requirements and joined Sheffield United for £500,000 in early 1996.

His travels then took him to Hibs, Raith Rovers, Ayr United, Carlisle United, Partick Thistle and finally to Alloa Athletic, as they chased and ultimately won promotion from the Second Division. He then retired as a player, and has since worked as a pundit for STV on their Scotsport highlights programme, of which he is now main presenter alongside Grant Stott, as well as writing a witty and perceptive column for the *Sunday Mail* newspaper.

WILLIE WALLACE

Born: Kirkintilloch, 23 June 1940
Celtic career: 1966 to 1971
Appearances and goals:

League		FA Cup		Lg Cup		Europe	
A	**G**	**A**	**G**	**A**	**G**	**A**	**G**
135/6	88	25/2	12	31/5	21	24/2	13

Total appearances: 215/15
Total goals: 134
League Championships: 1966-67; 19567-68; 1968-69; 1969-70; 1970-71
Scottish Cup: 1966-67; 1968-69; 1970-71
League Cup: 1967-68; 1968-69
European Cup: 1966-67
Honours: 7 Scotland caps

Jock Stein signed Willie Wallace from Hearts after competing with Rangers for his signature in 1966. At the time, the player, known as 'Wispy', was unhappy at Tynecastle over his wages and was considering leaving the country, and had made enquiries about emigrating to Canada.

He started his career with Stenhousemuir in 1958, before moving to Raith Rovers a year later. It was in Kirkcaldy that he developed a reputation as a top-class goal poacher, his skills being rewarded with Scottish League representative honours. His form attracted attention from larger clubs, and in April 1961, Hearts paid £15,000 to take him to Edinburgh.

The increased pressure for success at Tynecastle—where he had replaced the 'Golden Vision', Alex Young—initially curtailed his goalscoring exploits, but by 1962-63 he was fully settled into manager Tommy Walker's team style and topped the scoring charts for the next four seasons. After netting a hat-trick in a 4-0 League Cup semi-final defeat of St Johnstone, he went on to help Hearts win the final. His best season in terms of goals scored was 1963-64 when he netted 30 goals, going on to find the net 158 times in 277 games before Celtic secured his services.

At £29,000, he was the most expensive of Jock Stein's Lisbon Lions, the famous Celtic team that won the European Cup in 1967, having netted twice in the semi-final first leg win against Dukla Prague. He also hit another brace in that season's Scottish Cup Final defeat of Aberdeen. He capped a memorable season by also playing for Scotland in their memorable 3-2 defeat of World Champions England at Wembley.

Wallace won a League Championship winners' medal in each season he was at the Parkhead club, three Scottish Cup and two League Cup winners' medals. The only blemish in his time with the club was a disappointing 2-1 defeat to Feyenoord in the 1970 European Cup Final. His goal against Waterford after only 18 seconds is the club's quickest, and also its 100th in European football.

Wallace and his Celtic team-mate John Hughes were sold to Crystal Palace in 1971 for a combined fee of £30,000. Neither enjoyed great success at Selhurst Park, and Wallace was back in Scotland with Dumbarton less than a year later. As his career wound down, he moved to Australia in 1975 to play for Apia, where he won two league titles before returning to Scotland again to a coaching position at Dundee. When this role ended he returned to Apia as coach, eventually settling in Sydney and starting his own sports shop in Mount Druitt.

JOCK WEIR

Born: Fauldhouse, 20 October 1923
Died: 4 January 2003
Celtic career: 1948 to 1952
Appearances and goals:

League		FA Cup		Lg Cup		Europe	
A	G	A	G	A	G	A	G
80	26	15	9	10	2	-	-

Total appearances: 105
Total goals: 37
Scottish Cup: 1950-51

Versatile forward Jock Weir spent a relatively brief period at Parkhead, but he will live forever in Celtic folklore as the player who scored a hat-trick to help the side avoid relegation!

Having begun his career with Leith Renton, Weir moved to Hibernian during the war, later 'guesting' for Cardiff City and Brighton and Hove Albion. When peacetime football resumed, Weir left Easter Road midway through the 1946-47 season to join Blackburn Rovers for a fee of £10,000. Even so, he ended that campaign as the Edinburgh club's leading scorer with 23 goals in all competitions.

He had spent just over a season at Ewood Park when Celtic paid a then club record fee of £7,000 to take Weir to Parkhead. A pacy and powerful forward, he made his debut for the Hoops in a Scottish Cup tie against Motherwell, a match Celtic won 1-0. A couple of months after putting pen to paper, Jock Weir saved the club from the distinct possibility of relegation by netting a hat-trick in a 3-2 defeat of Dundee at Dens Park, in what was the club's last league game of the 1947-48 season. A firm favourite thereafter with the Celtic faithful, he was at outside-right in the first side to lift a post-war Scottish Cup in 1951 as Motherwell were beaten 1-0 courtesy of a John McPhail goal.

A few days later he went on the club's tour of the United States. He was a member of the Celtic side that played Eintracht Frankfurt for the Schaeffer Trophy, when there was fighting both on the field and in the crowd. It is reported that Jock told his German marker Kudrass, 'I was paid two bob a day during the War to kill big ------s like you!'

Jock Weir and Northern Ireland international Charlie Tully were great mates. Charlie could never get over how Jock signed for Celtic and then spent a year and a half living in the Kenilworth Hotel at the club's expense. For Tully, this proved Jock Weir was that special something that Glaswegians call 'gallus'. In his book *Passed to You*, Tully said that, 'Whenever the boys were at a loose end, we would go to the hotel and order a meal and put it on Jock's room number. I don't know how the club could afford it, or how Jock never tumbled to our game.'

In October 1952, Weir and Celtic parted company, with the fast-raiding forward leaving to play for Falkirk. Later in that 1952-53 season, Weir scored for the Bairns in the famous Scottish Cup tie at Brockville in which Tully netted twice from a retaken corner-kick.

Weir later had brief spells with non-League Llanelli and Dumbarton before calling time on his illustrious playing career.

DEREK WHYTE

Born: Glasgow, 31 August 1968
Celtic career: 1985 to 1992
Appearances and goals:

League		FA Cup		Lg Cup		Europe	
A	G	A	G	A	G	A	G
211/5	7	26	0	18/1	0	15	1

Total appearances: 270/6
Total goals: 8
League Championships: 1985-86; 1987-88
Scottish Cup: 1987-88; 1988-89
Honours: 12 Scotland caps

Derek Whyte's impact as a defender for the Hoops was immediate, and he seemed destined for a great future as the Parkhead club's captain.

Having joined the club as a 16-year-old from the Celtic Boys Club, he was a defender with the greatest of promise, described as the new Billy McNeill. He made his Celtic debut in a 1-1 draw against League title favourites Hearts in February 1986, as Celtic surged up the table to take the title at the last gasp.

Whyte won another League Championship medal in 1987-88, a season in which he also won a Scottish Cup winners' medal as Celtic defeated Dundee United 2-1. He won another Scottish Cup winners' medal the following season as Celtic beat rivals Rangers 1-0. Joe Miller had just scored for the Hoops when Whyte cleared a Mark Walters shot off the line as the Light Blues pressed for an equaliser.

Towards the end of his time at Parkhead, Derek Whyte's form began to slump, and following a disagreement over terms, he was allowed to join Middlesbrough for a fee of £900,000.

Whyte had made his full international debut against Belgium in 1988, going on to make 12 appearances—only one of which saw him on the losing side. He was also part of a Scotland defence that didn't concede a goal in nine of those games, including his first seven appearances for the national side.

He was a virtual ever-present in his few seasons on Teesside, helping them win the First Division Championship in 1994-95, and after some sterling displays the following season as the club returned to the Premiership, won selection for Scotland's 1996 European Championship squad. In 1996-97, he played an important role in Boro's two cup runs, and though the club lost their top flight status, it wasn't for the want of trying on Derek Whyte's part.

After five seasons at Middlesbrough, Whyte, whose strong running out of defence along with good distribution were the main features of his play, joined Aberdeen. He was soon appointed captain at Pittodrie, and spent four years in the Granite City before leaving to continue his career with Partick Thistle. Along with Gerry Britton, Whyte was appointed joint player-manager of the Jags when Gerry Collins was sacked in November 2003. He later gave up the game as a player to concentrate on management, but was sacked by Partick in January 2005.

Derek Whyte is now a pundit with ART Sport in Dubai, providing the expats with high quality coverage of the English Premiership and the UEFA Champions' League.

PAUL WILSON

Born: Milngavie, 23 November 1950
Celtic career: 1967 to 1978
Appearances and goals:

League		FA Cup		Lg Cup		Europe	
A	G	A	G	A	G	A	G
117/14	29	41/7	13	11/4	4	16/4	6

Total appearances: 185/29
Total goals: 52

League Championships: 1976-77
Scottish Cup: 1974-75; 1976-77
League Cup: 1974-75
Honours: 1 Scotland cap

Son of a Scottish father and Indian mother, Paul Wilson was a spectacular raider with speed, control and a powerful shot, yet though there were high hopes that one day he would be an all-time Celtic great in succession to Johnstone or Lennox, he was unable consistently to command a regular place in the Hoops team.

Having joined Celtic from Maryhill Juniors, his first few seasons at Parkhead were disappointing, and it wasn't really until 1974-75 that he won a regular place at outside-left in the Celtic side. That season was the first that he hadn't started in the reserves, and his form throughout the campaign saw him win full international honours for Scotland against Spain in Valencia. Coming off the bench to replace Kenny Burns, he was instrumental in the making of Scotland's goal scored by Joe Jordan, in a game that ended all-square at 1-1.

That 1974-75 season, Wilson won both League Cup and Scottish Cup winners' medals, scoring in both finals—he scored once as Celtic beat Hibernian 6-3 to lift the League Cup and netted twice as the Hoops defeated Airdrie 3-1 to win the Scottish Cup. That season he also scored with a brilliant header against Rangers in the Dryborough Cup, and then gave a magnificent display of running, shooting and control against the same opposition in the Glasgow Cup Final, played to celebrate the city's 800th birthday, scoring both Celtic's goals in a 2-2 draw. There is no doubt that Paul Wilson would invariably raise his game if Rangers were the opposition!

Though he made way when Alfie Conn arrived at Parkhead in March 1977, he was still Jock Stein's first choice for the Parkhead club's assault on Europe the following season. However, on the domestic scene, Celtic had a disastrous campaign, and Wilson, who had scored 52 goals in 214 games, was allowed to leave, and, in September 1978, he joined Motherwell for a fee of £50,000.

His stay at Fir Park was brief, and the following summer he moved on to Partick Thistle. On leaving the Jags, he went into junior football, playing for Blantyre Celtic. It was while he was playing here that John Hughes capped him for Junior Scotland against the Republic of Ireland at Irvine Meadow in October 1980.

At the end of his playing career, he became coach to Drumchapel Amateurs.

MACIEJ ZURAWSKI

Born: Poznan, Poland, 12 September 1976
Celtic career: 2005 to 2007
Appearances and goals:

League		FA Cup		Lg Cup		Europe	
A	**G**	**A**	**G**	**A**	**G**	**A**	**G**
42/11	22	1/1	3	4/1	5	6/1	0

Total appearances: 53/14
Total goals: 30
League Championships: 2005-06; 2006-07
Scottish Cup: 2006-07
League Cup: 2005-06
Honours: 64 Poland caps

Celtic finally completed the £2 million signing of Polish international striker Maciej Zurawski from Wisla Krakow in the summer of 2005, after a lengthy courtship on the Parkhead outfit's part. He opted to move to Celtic rather than sign for Trabzonspor, who had also been keen on securing the player's services.

He had started his career at Warta Poznan, where his father was the first team coach, but his first two seasons with the club saw them suffer successive relegations to II Liga and then III Liga. In 1997 Warta returned to II Liga but were relegated again that same season. Zurawski then parted company with the club, moving across the town to join rivals Lech Poznan. It was here that he won the first of his 58 Polish caps when playing in a 3-1 defeat of Slovakia.

In the summer of 2000, Zurawski was on the move again, this time to Wisla Krakow. After a disappointing start, he helped the club win the 2000-01 Polish Championship and League Cup, and the following season was top scorer with 21 goals in 27 games as the club retained the Cup.

With Zurawski playing a big part in the club's successes, they won the Polish Championship for the next three successive seasons, and the Polish Cup again in 2002-03. After many rumours of an impending move to a league in Western Europe, Zurawski was sold to Celtic.

After signing a three-year contract, he inherited the No.7 shirt from former Celtic legend Henrik Larsson. Known as 'Magic' by the Celtic fans, he proved in his first season at Parkhead that he had an eye for goal.

Having scored the opening goal for the Hoops in the 3-0 League Cup Final win over Dunfermline Athletic, he went on to score 16 league goals in 22 starts, including four in the match against Dunfermline Athletic in February 2006 as Celtic set a new Scottish Premier League record by winning 8-1. Not surprisingly he was voted the SPL Player of the Month!

Zurawski was hampered by injuries in 2006-07, but whenever selected he demonstrated that he still had an eye for goal. Though not as prolific in the League, he set the club on their way in the Tennants Scottish Cup by netting twice in the opening eight minutes of the 4-0 defeat of Dumbarton. Celtic fans will be hoping that this most popular of players can stay injury-free this season as the club aim for a third Scottish Premier League Championship in succession.

CELTIC 100 HEROES TOP TENS

LEAGUE

APPEARANCES

1	Paul McStay	509/6
2	Billy McNeill	486
3=	Roy Aitken	483
	Packie Bonner	483
5	Danny McGrain	433/8
6	Bobby Evans	385
7	Peter Grant	338/26
8	Tommy Burns	324/32
9	Bobby Lennox	297/50
10	Jimmy Johnstone	298/10

GOALS

1	Henrik Larsson	174
2	Bobby Lennox	168
3	Steve Chalmers	156
4	John Hughes	116
5	Kenny Dalglish	112
6	Brian McClair	99
7	Dixie Deans	89
8	Willie Wallace	88
9	John Hartson	87
10	Charlie Nicholas	85

CELTIC 100 HEROES TOP TENS

SCOTTISH CUP

APPEARANCES

1	Billy McNeill	94
2	Paul McStay	66
3	Bobby Evans	64
4	Danny McGrain	60
5	Bertie Peacock	56
6=	Roy Aitken	55
	Packie Bonner	55
8	Bobby Murdoch	53
9	Bobby Lennox	47/5
10	Jimmy Johnstone	47/1

GOALS

1	Bobby Lennox	31
2	Steve Chalmers	29
3	John Hughes	25
4	Henrik Larsson	23
5	Dixie Deans	18
6	John McPhail	17
7	Neil Mochan	16
8=	Harry Hood	13
	Frank McGarvey	13
	Bobby Murdoch	13
	Paul Wilson	13

CELTIC 100 HEROES TOP TENS

LEAGUE CUP

APPEARANCES

1	Billy McNeill	138
2	Bobby Lennox	107/14
3	Danny McGrain	105/1
4	Jimmy Johnstone	87/5
5	Bobby Evans	88
6=	Bobby Murdoch	84
	Roy Aitken	82/2
8	Bertie Peacock	80
9	Tommy Gemmell	74
10	Tommy Burns	70/1

GOALS

1	Bobby Lennox	63
2	John Hughes	38
3	Kenny Dalglish	35
4	Steve Chalmers	31
5=	Bobby Collins	26
	Charlie Nicholas	26
7=	Harry Hood	24
	Joe McBride	24
9=	Jimmy Johnstone	21
	Willie Wallace	21

CELTIC 100 HEROES TOP TENS

EUROPE

APPEARANCES

1	Billy McNeill	69
2	Bobby Lennox	54/12
3	Jimmy Johnstone	63/1
4	Henrik Larsson	58
5=	Bobby Murdoch	54
	Danny McGrain	53/1
7	Neil Lennon	52/1
8	Jackie McNamara	43/9
9=	Tommy Gemmell	51
	Stiliyan Petrov	49/2

GOALS

1	Henrik Larsson	35
2=	Jimmy Johnstone	16
	Chris Sutton	16
4	Bobby Lennox	14
5=	Steve Chalmers	13
	Willie Wallace	13
7	Harry Hood	12
8=	Tommy Gemmell	11
	Bobby Murdoch	11
10	John Hughes	10

CELTIC 100 HEROES TOP TENS

OVERALL

APPEARANCES

1	Billy McNeill	787
2	Paul McStay	672/6
3	Roy Aitken	667/2
4	Danny McGrain	651/10
5	Packie Bonner	642
6	Bobby Lennox	505/81
7	Bobby Evans	537
8	Jimmy Johnstone	495/17
9	Tommy Burns	464/41
10	Bobby Murdoch	478/4

GOALS

1	Bobby Lennox	276
2	Henrik Larsson	242
3	Steve Chalmers	229
4	John Hughes	189
5	Kenny Dalglish	167
6	Willie Wallace	134
7	Jimmy Johnstone	130
8	Charlie Nicholas	125
9	Dixie Deans	124
10	Harry Hood	123